Young

2004 POETRY

ONCE UPON A RHYME

IMAGINATION FOR
A NEW GENERATION

Northern England Vol II
Edited by Chris Hallam

 Young**Writers**

First published in Great Britain in 2004 by:
Young Writers
Remus House
Coltsfoot Drive
Peterborough
PE2 9JX
Telephone: 01733 890066
Website: www.youngwriters.co.uk

SB ISBN 1 84460 505 1

Foreword

Young Writers was established in 1991 and has been passionately devoted to the promotion of reading and writing in children and young adults ever since. The quest continues today. Young Writers remains as committed to engendering the fostering of burgeoning poetic and literary talent as ever.

This year's Young Writers competition has proven as vibrant and dynamic as ever and we are delighted to present a showcase of the best poetry from across the UK. Each poem has been carefully selected from a wealth of *Once Upon A Rhyme* entries before ultimately being published in this, our twelfth primary school poetry series.

Once again, we have been supremely impressed by the overall high quality of the entries we have received. The imagination, energy and creativity which has gone into each young writer's entry made choosing the best poems a challenging and often difficult but ultimately hugely rewarding task - the general high standard of the work submitted amply vindicating this opportunity to bring their poetry to a larger appreciative audience.

We sincerely hope you are pleased with our final selection and that you will enjoy *Once Upon A Rhyme Northern England Vol II* for many years to come.

Contents

James Baker (11)   17
Kassandra Starling (11)   18
Dannii Egan (10)   18
James Connor (10)   19
Lisa Surtees (10)   20
Ryan Whittington (11)   20
Katie Turner (10)   21
Claire Louise Smith (11)   21
Richard Creed (10)   22
Daniel Simpson (10)   22
Jordan Pegman (10)   23
Jack Dunn (10)   23
Sarah Barnes (10)   24
Kathryn Bowley (11)   24
Rebecca Clymo (11)   25
Khyle Douglas Fryer (10)   25
Joanna Maddison (10)   26
Tasmin Johnson (11)   26
David Griffiths (11)   27
Philip Milburn (11)   28
Patrick Bonnar (10)   28
Stephanie Louise Bell (11)   29
Jack Mather (11)   29
Anthony Jackson (10)   30
Adelle Bailey (11)   31

Hylton Red House Primary School, Sunderland

Abbie Hartley (10)   31
Louise Kelly (11)   32
Luke Matthews (10)   32
Barry Small (11)   32
Faye Richardson (11)   33
Samantha Jones (11)   33
Amy King (11)   33
Sara Hodgson (11)   34

John F Kennedy Primary School, Washington

Nathan Gaffney (11)   34
Laura Thompson (10)   35
Rebecca Oliver (8)   35
Abby Spalding (9)   36

Name	Score
Sarah Cobain (7)	58
Natalie Brown (11)	59
Nicola Freckleton (11)	59
Emma Scott (10)	60
Kimberley Coulter (9)	60
Michael Grist (9)	61
James Thompson (11)	62
Naomi Andersson (8)	62
Sheryl Hedley (9)	63
Christopher Barton (8)	63
Shannan Mullen (9)	64
Megan Laing (9)	64
Benjamin Butterfield (11)	65
Hannah Wylie (9)	65
Kelsey Duncan (8)	66
Philippa Ogden (10)	66
Michael Watkis (9)	67
Stephanie Ellwood (9)	67
Stacey Harris (10)	68
Jenny Cawson (10)	68
Danielle Roberts (9)	69
Sarah Bradley (10)	69
Gabrielle Rawson (8)	70
Reece McMann (10)	70
Rhys Buckham (9)	71
Daryl McMahon (7)	71
Liam Noble (9)	72
Christopher Johnson (9)	72
Alexander Maddison (10)	73
Jade Walmsley (9)	74
Natalie Taylor (10)	74
Sophie Jordan (9)	75
Alex Hair (9)	75
Amy Richardson (8)	76
Brent Bradbury (8)	77
Emma Brewer (9)	78
Victoria Whitehead (10)	78
Parisa Asl (10)	79
Sophie Henderson (7)	79
Hannah Thompson (11)	80
Jordan Dixon (10)	80
Lauren Southern (10)	81

Charlotte McIntosh (8)	81
Victoria Graham (11)	82
Jordan Foley (10)	82
Robert Lloyd (10)	83
Rhys Duffner (8)	83
Victoria Doran (9)	84
Craig Foster (7)	84
Jordan Batey (10)	85
Jack Short (7)	85
Christina Savage (10)	86
Cristal Robinson (9)	86
Emma Povey (7)	87
Faye Chenery (7)	87
Samantha Derrick (9)	88
Kirstie Sloan (9)	88
Andy Johnson (10)	89
Natasha Cullerton (10)	89
Chloe Hesketh (10)	90
James Reay (11)	90
Emily Allan (11)	91
Laura Doran (9)	91
Leanne Markham (11)	92
Sarah Warde (9)	92
Sophie Sanderson (10)	93
Jade Illingworth (11)	93
Ka Ho Law (11)	94
Ross Spalding (11)	94
Jennifer Donnison (11)	95
Daisy Wells (10)	96
Jonathan Edwards (10)	96
Danielle Stone (11)	97
Dean Finch (10)	97
Niall Mullen (10)	98
Kirsty Dodd (11)	99

Ludworth Primary School, Ludworth

Laura Conley (9)	99
Scott Carter (10)	100
Daniel Rowlinson (8)	100
Rachel Stabler (10)	101
Liam Turnbull (7)	101

Our Lady Of The Rosary RC Primary School, Peterlee

Redesdale Primary School, Wallsend

Helen Fong (11)	136
Sophie Watson (11)	136
Amy Sill (11)	136
Michael Woodmass (10)	137
Emily Watson (11)	137
James Clements (11)	137
Lee Turnbull (11)	138
Thomas Lapworth (10)	138

Ryhope Junior School, Sunderland

Georgia Creasy (8)	139
Kristi Henson (8)	139
Amy Hibbert (7)	140
Becky Clark (8)	140
Abby Cooper (10)	140
Allison Brettell (10)	141
Stacey Sinclair (7)	141
Lewis Anthony Storey (8)	141
James Hartley (9)	142
Hannah Barkel (8)	142
Ivan Godfrey (9)	142
Adam Kitching (9)	143
Nathan Riley (10)	143
Rebekah Ruddock (10)	143
Bethany Allen (8)	144
Demi Procter (8)	144
Glyn Lamb (8)	145
Sarah Halsall (9)	145
Melainey Camsey	146
Robyn Atkinson (9)	146
Kyle Dixon (9)	146
Holly Mclaughlin (9)	147
Luke Hammal (8)	147
Daniel Dunn (9)	147
Connor Usher (8)	148
Brandon Lisle (8)	148
Zoe Knebel (8)	149

St Joseph's RC (VA) Primary School, Stanley

Shaun Broadley (10)	149
Steven Pendleton (10)	150

Adam Close (10)	150
Amy Sinclair (10)	150
Stephen Cowan (11)	151
Ashlee Richardson (10)	151
Katie Rimington (10)	151
Derek Weelands (10)	152
Christopher Pye (10)	152
Coral Brough (10)	152
Jonathon Hall (10)	153
Brendan Faherty (10)	153
Nicola Wall (10)	154
Sean Waite (11)	154
Lorenzo Fella (11)	154
Emma Donnelly (10)	155
Maxine Hamflett (11)	155
Michael Handy (11)	155
Chloe Costello (10)	156
Aaron Waite (10)	156
Megan Scott (10)	157

St Mary's RC Primary School, Sunderland

Abbie Scarlett (11)	157
Abbie Kelf (10)	158
Holly Raper (11)	158
Anthony Callaghan (9)	159
Eszter Soos (10)	159
Rebecca Adams (9)	160
Liam Walker (10)	160
Niamh Baldasera (10)	161
Simon French (9)	161
Joseph Dunn (10)	162
Anthony Lewis (9)	162
Joshua Brown (11)	163
Kate Stenger (10)	163
Jessica Pye (10)	164
Craig MacDonald (9)	164
Ashleigh Simpson (9)	165
Rebecca Prestwood (11)	165
Melanie Golding (9)	166
Matthew Harrison (10)	166
Rebecca Hughes (9)	166

Francesca Kelly (10)	167
Emily Bird (9)	167
Lizzie Fetherston (11)	168
Bret McCarthy (10)	168
Jason Gray (9)	169
Lucy Farrell (10)	169
Sophie Fenwick (10)	169
Cameron Phillips (10)	170
Laila Mahmoodshahi (10)	170
Holly Smith (9)	171
Georgina Currie (10)	171
Matthew Barber (10)	172
Katherine Lamb (10)	172
Josh Kelly (9)	173
Sarah Forrest (10)	173
Christie Bainbridge (10)	174
Matthew Banks (10)	174
Caitlin Hindmarsh (9)	174
Rebecca Smith (9)	175
William Lewis (9)	176

St Patrick's RC Primary School, Ryhope

Alex Tang (7)	176
Charlie Addison (7)	177

St William's RCVA Primary School, Trimdon Village

Louise Gardiner (9)	177
Olivia Dowling (8)	178
Jane Snowball (8)	178
Sarah Hawley (10)	179
Shannon Turnbull (9)	179
Robert Moran (9)	180
Tom Robertshaw (9)	180
Rachael Donnachie (10)	181
Claire Harnett (9)	181
Emily Ruth Lovett (11)	182
Kate Hewitt (8)	182
Stephanie Storey (11)	183
Nicole Peters (9)	183
Sophie Fellows (8)	184
Grace Robinson (9)	184

Witherwack Primary School, Sunderland

Danielle Louise Steel (10)	205
Amy Leadbitter (8)	205
James Stoddart (8)	206
Laura Jayne Steel (7)	206

The Poems

I Love Our School Parachute

I love our school parachute,
The colours glow,
Like a shining rainbow.

And when there is a gust of wind,
It flutters in the air,
Like a gigantic bird flapping its wings.

When the sun comes out,
It drifts about,
Like the world spinning round slowly.

And when I go underneath,
I feel warm,
Like a bird in a nest.

When I hold it up,
Children run under it,
And sometimes it goes down like a bird landing.

I love our school parachute.

Lance Russell (8)
Bilsdale Midcable Chop Gate CE School, Middlesbrough

The Owl And The Pussy Cat Continued

(Inspired by 'The Owl And The Pussy Cat' by Edward Lear)

They walked by the sea, and had cockles for tea,
    Sitting side by side on the sand,
When they were done, Owl said, 'Let's have some fun,'
    So they danced to the great silver band.
Then they went home to a house of their own,
    From his pocket, Owl pulled out a key.
He said to his wife, 'I'll spend my life,
    Caring for you and me,
You and me,
You and me,
    Caring for you and me.'

Keziah Brass (8)
Bilsdale Midcable Chop Gate CE School, Middlesbrough

Cats

Cats are a ball of fluff,
Cats have sharp claws,
They have long whiskers,
They have long tails.

Some cats are *big*,
Some cats are *small*.

Mason Fawcett (7)
Bilsdale Midcable Chop Gate CE School, Middlesbrough

I Love Our School Parachute

I love our school parachute,
The colours are big and bold,
And stand out against the green grass.

When the breeze comes,
It lifts up into the sky,
Like a vulture stalking its prey.

When you sit underneath,
It is like Joseph's multicoloured coat,
Flying about you.

I love our school parachute.

Paige Brundall (8)
Bilsdale Midcable Chop Gate CE School, Middlesbrough

Ghosts

Ghosts scare people,
Ghosts are white and squeegee,
Ghosts haunt,
Ghosts fly,
Ghosts appear in old castles and crooked houses,
Ghosts disappear at dawn.

Lauren Hugill (7)
Bilsdale Midcable Chop Gate CE School, Middlesbrough

Playground Rap

Let's all go
The school playground.
Lots of children,
Lots of sound.
All the classes
Playing around.
Lance and Edward
Running about,
Lauren and Joe
Chasing a ball.
Let's all go
To the school playground.

Edward Sutcliffe (8)
Bilsdale Midcable Chop Gate CE School, Middlesbrough

I Love Our School Parachute

I love our school parachute
Because it is like a tree blowing
When we play in it.

When the wind blows
The parachute flaps
Like a flying eagle.

I hear the birds sing
In the breeze
And the sun shines down.

When the sun shines
That's when I love it best,
Our parachute is like a rainbow.

I love our school parachute.

Joe Brown (10)
Bilsdale Midcable Chop Gate CE School, Middlesbrough

The Owl And The Pussy Cat Continued

(Inspired by 'The Owl And The Pussy Cat' by Edward Lear)

They walked by the sea and went home for tea,
   And sat in the garden to dine,
When they had fed, Pussy sat back and said,
   'Oh Owl I'm so glad you're mine.'
Owl strummed his guitar, 'How pretty you are,'
   He sang to his wife Pussy Cat
'I'm so glad we're together, hopefully forever,'
   He said, on the chair as he sat,
   He sat,
   He sat,
He said, on the chair as he sat.

Joshua Smith (10)
Bilsdale Midcable Chop Gate CE School, Middlesbrough

Boarding School

B is for how boring it will be,
O is for orange cake I have sneaked,
A is for apples, I've got two,
R is for reading, writing and more,
D is for doing all my work,
 I is for ignoring everyone else,
N is for not knowing what will happen,
G is for going home in 12 weeks!

S is for the peculiar smell,
C is for the cold colour of the cane,
H is for this being my new home for a while,
O is for the other children stuck here too,
O is for the other people - feeling the same as me!
L is for me being alone.

Bethany Laidlaw (11)
Dene House Primary School, Peterlee

Boarding School

B is for the nasty boarding school, no one likes,
O is for the old headmaster, who owns the place,
A is for a tiny room I hate to sleep in,
R is for the radio we have to listen to,
D is for the disgusting dinners - we have to eat,
I is for the I don't want lessons - I don't, I don't!
N is for nanny or maiden,
G is for giant headmasters and teachers!

S is for my strict teacher, Mr Spice,
C is for candy in my tuck box,
H is for howl, which I do all the time,
O is for orange, again in my tuck box,
O is for owl, I hear all night long,
L is for a lullaby, I sing to myself.

Emma Malcolm (10)
Dene House Primary School, Peterlee

Carnival

At the carnival people danced and played,
While others, just watched and gazed,
People screaming, shouting on the rides,
'Be careful' a young person advised.

Go for ice creams, candyfloss too,
Others all dashing to the loo,
At night-time, the rides still go on,
Teenagers drinking, drunk, drunk, and gone!

And for now it's time to pack away,
The bands stop their play,
And then within just one day,
The rides are really, really far away.

Jade Goundry (11)
Dene House Primary School, Peterlee

The Witch

Soaring through the moonlit sky,
A black and gruesome witch does fly,
That's when she saw it, in her glance,
Now to all her friends she would rant.

Only one thing left for her potion,
And that was the frog's tongue lotion!
That's she'd have to make herself,
She looked upon her rotten shelf.

She had the things she would need,
So she could finish her evil deed!
Now it was ready, it was complete,
She drank it, then sat upon her seat.

She began to grow, she couldn't stop,
Began to have visions of going pop!
The story of what happened that day,
Well, that's a price she'd have to pay!

Amy Kennedy (11)
Dene House Primary School, Peterlee

Mountains

M is for Mount Everest,
O is for oxygen, which we use too much,
U is for us, you and me as a team,
N is for the narrow ledges and tracks,
T is for the very top of the mountain,
A is for an avalanche, waiting to happen,
I is for icy slopes waiting for me,
N is for nobody reaching the top,
S is for lots of snow.

Scott James (10)
Dene House Primary School, Peterlee

The Blessing

While I was waking up that morning,
The thought I thought, just started dawning,
Today was the day of my parent's blessing,
It's just like a second wedding.

I told my mum, 'Wake up, wake up!'
I told my dad, 'Wake up, wake up!'
Natasha followed me close by,
I was that excited - I thought I would die!

I got dressed at 9 o'clock,
Hairdressers at 10 o'clock,
My hair looked absolutely great,
It was half-past twelve - we were nearly late!

We rushed home, as fast as we could,
We should have gone earlier, we should!
We got dressed into our dresses,
Both our rooms were utter messes!

Round the roundabout we go,
Up to the church, our nerves weren't low,
Pull up at the church, walk down the aisle,
People stared at us a while.

The vicar speaks - my dad replies,
People sigh, some even cry!
We sing a hymn - we all must stand
My mum puts a ring on my dad's hand.

Now it is Mum's turn to speak,
Her knees had gone extremely weak,
We sing another hymn - Mum's fave,
This is the day that we should save.

My parents cutting the cake with a knife,
Ended the best memory of my life!

Bethany Miller (11)
Dene House Primary School, Peterlee

Waterfalls

As I looked I blinked my eyes,
As they nearly touched the skies.
You could just hear a splashing sound,
Under the waterfalls - lots to be found.

And then I went into a boat,
I didn't worry - because it would float.
We sailed so far on the lake,
It really kept my mum awake.

Our boat sailed under a waterfall,
Mum really worried - it wasn't small!
We came out - I had freezing breath,
And I was also - freezing to death!

Jumping onto the platform,
I got a soft towel to keep me warm.
Then I walked along the path,
Very happily went into the cafe.

Steven Wheatley (11)
Dene House Primary School, Peterlee

Everest

Everest is the highest mountain,
It is very tall,
When you climb up to the top,
The world seems ever so small.

The Himalayan mountain range,
Of which Everest is the highest,
Runs on for miles and miles,
Ever upward to the skies.

The other mountains in the Himalayas
Are Kathmandu and Nagarkot,
Not reaching the height of Everest,
The tallest mountain of all.

Alex Matthews (11)
Dene House Primary School, Peterlee

Harry Potter

Magical, mysterious
What will happen next?
Moving stairs
Plus lots of thrilling dares.

Voldermort the enemy,
Who Harry will come to face,
Hermione might be clever,
But will she be there forever?

Ron thinks there's always worse to come,
Usually he is out, if there is!
Snape and the other teachers are always very strict,
But it doesn't stop Harry, from playing tricks!

So the end has come,
And Harry has finally won,
The poignant battle of pain,
Now he is with the Dursley's again!

Amy Cartney (11)
Dene House Primary School, Peterlee

Mountains

Mountains so big,
Mountains so tall,
Everest the highest,
The tallest of them all.

When you look ahead,
The sky is so blue,
'Look at those beautiful sights,' I said,
She said, 'Hey I see them too!'

I really couldn't look down,
She looked down, pulled a frown,
She just stood there gazing,
I really thought it was amazing!

Amie Mackie (11)
Dene House Primary School, Peterlee

Lightwater Valley

I went to Lightwater Valley,
With Summer School - if you ask.
It was really great,
I went on the Mexican Hat.

We went on the pirate ship,
Suzanne was very nearly sick!
It started to rain,
Lucky Vicky didn't get wet.

Mexican Hat, pirate ship,
What shall we go on next?
I know, the go-karts,
Oh no, too long a queue!

Instead we went on the log flume,
It wasn't a very long wait,
Kate and I sat at the front,
We were wet right through when it stopped,
Because it was a very sudden drop!

Fiona Rachael Brown (10)
Dene House Primary School, Peterlee

Tuck Box

T is for my tuck box with personal things,
U is for unpleasant teachers,
C is for children doing hard work,
K is for kicking my leather ball.

B is for bullies that pick on little people,
O is for my soft, juicy oranges,
X is for my excellent toy car.

Craig Hancock (11)
Dene House Primary School, Peterlee

Mountains

Jagged edges, rocky peaks,
Rough sides, big leaps,
Tall heights, low jumps,
Huge, grey, rocky lumps.

One step, two, off we go,
Hiking boots tread in the snow,
Oh, there's still some hope in me,
When I reach the top, I'll shout with glee!

Huff, puff, deep breaths now,
Nearly there, I don't know how,
Just be careful, you don't slip,
You'll drop down, just like a pip.

Only two more steps to go,
My feet are numb, can't feel a toe,
Yes, yes, I've hit the peak,
Now I only want to sleep!

Laura Martin (10)
Dene House Primary School, Peterlee

Tuck Box

T is for my tuck box and all the teachers inside,
U is for my uncaring mother, sitting at home,
C is for my catapult which I have made,
K is for kids crying, who I hit with my catapult.

B is for bossy head teacher, who tells me off,
O is for objects that I get at school,
X is for extras, which I sneaked with me.

Christopher Hall Hogarth (10)
Dene House Primary School, Peterlee

Boxing

Fists swinging all over the shop,
I take a haymaker, the nose goes pop.
Here comes a left, then a right,
The sparring round turns into a fight.

My most powerful shot goes in his eye,
He falls to the ground - ready to cry,
A hand slap, the mat 1, 2, 3,
The number 10 comes eventually.

I do some training on the punching bag,
I swing it hard, it hits my dad,
My fists swing on the speed ball,
I knew soon it would fall.

I skip fast with the skipping ropes,
'It's really good how I cope,'
I get driven home, in the bright red car,
I tell my mam, I love to spar.

Lee Scurr (11)
Dene House Primary School, Peterlee

Spain

Where I am, is very tame,
Maybe I'll go back to Spain,
This time I hope it doesn't rain,
Like it did - last year in Spain.

Maybe now I'll get a car,
To ride along the roads of tar,
I will take it to the shops,
To get some food and lots of pop.

I will go to the sandy beach,
Where I'll eat a lovely peach,
Or I might swim in the sea,
Take my sisters along with me!

Stearman Harle (11)
Dene House Primary School, Peterlee

Mountains

Climbing high, reaching far,
Have no clue, of where we are.
Looking up in the sky,
Would be a bad fall, we are so high!
Feeling weak, we must go on,
We find a cave, which is so long,
We stay there for one night,
Then go to climb a higher height.
Won't give up now, we're near the top,
But no it's just a break - a piece of rock!
Now it ends we're at the top,
We did it, but it took a lot!
Climbing high, reaching far,
Have no clue of where we are,
Look up into the sky,
Now if we fall, we could die!

Alex Dobson (10)
Dene House Primary School, Peterlee

Boarding School

B is for boarding school, where I went,
O is for one boy, who kept a frog in his box,
A is for all the treasure I took in my box,
R is for the racing car, which I wind up,
D is for half a dozen lead soldiers,
I is for interesting things I took,
N is for never seeing my parents for long,
G is for the giant headmaster.

S is for the string I took,
C is for the box of conjuring tricks that I would use,
H is for how many fried eggs will I have,
O is for how organised I will be,
O is for other people I would meet,
L is for the lid of my tuck box.

Kate Fisher (10)
Dene House Primary School, Peterlee

Rachel

My sister was being born
And it was close to dawn
My mum was hotting up
While I drank out of my favourite cup.

Then she was two
There was not much to do
Then she was four
And she loved the bear Pooh!

Now she's six
I'm in a mix
She's so cute
She loves to play the flute!

She's now at school
And all the boys drool
At her cute, little face
She's starting to eat liquorice lace!
Love you Rachel!

Katharine Pounder (10)
Dene House Primary School, Peterlee

Skiing

S is for all the snowboarders flying past me,
K is for feeling like King of the World when I'm skiing,
I is for I nearly fell over my first time,
I is for interesting things I see as I fly down the Piste,
N is for not wanting to fall down,
G is for getting to the bottom safely.

Ben Farrell (10)
Dene House Primary School, Peterlee

Mountains

Mountains belong to their own ranges
But also have many dangers,
I try to climb up the three peaks
As we go up, I feel so weak.

As we go up to the top
I feel as though we shouldn't stop,
Leaving footprints in the snow
I wish I could just go, go, go.

Climbing, climbing to the top
I really, really cannot stop,
Just a little way to go
Frostbite on all my toes.

I am now at the top
I'm pleased I didn't give in and stop,
Now it's time to set off home
And it's now time to end the poem.

Amy Laverick (11)
Dene House Primary School, Peterlee

Mountains

M is for melting snow,
O is for oxygen that is hard to get,
U is for underneath the snow,
N is for narrow mountain paths,
T is for tiny rocks - that make me slip,
A is for all the slippery snow,
I is for icicles that fall from the rocks,
N is for not any pop to drink,
S is for snow on the mountain tops.

Hannah-Leigh Westgarth (10)
Dene House Primary School, Peterlee

The Stadium Of Light

Last Thursday we went on our trip
Our trip was to the Stadium of Light,
The bus left at 9.30
I couldn't wait for it to arrive,
When we arrived we went in the classroom
We learnt a bit about the club in there,
We then went into the changing rooms,
We touched the shirts in there.
The away changing rooms weren't that nice
Pea green and blue were the colours,
We then went into the stadium
49,000 seats in all.
We sat on the badge and could see the
Stadium and all around.
Once our day had ended
I didn't really want to go.

Natasha Scott (10)
Easington Colliery Primary School, Peterlee

Football

Football is the greatest thing
When you play it, it's like you are king
And as that small hard ball comes to you
You kick it and it flies up like a balloon
We all like to do a trick
And we all like to do a flick
After half-time we do our best
And we clear out all the rest,
There goes that win to our team
Then we have that break and go for an ice cream
And all the other games we played,
The keeper couldn't save one shot,
And at last our team is so hot.

Lee Glaister (11)
Easington Colliery Primary School, Peterlee

Trip To Sunderland

It was a school trip today
I got up and got dressed
I said 'Finally a trip hooray!'
When I got to school, I said,
'I think this is the best.'

We got on the bus
We sat and started to chat
We got off the bus and stretched like a crust
Then we saw the black cats.

We went in a class and sat down
We had a test
We got no points so we started to frown
David's team was the best.

We had our packed lunch
I got a sweet
Me and Lauren started to munch
It was a treat.

Sophie Kenney (10)
Easington Colliery Primary School, Peterlee

The Black Cats

S underland the red and whites,
U nited with Mick MacCarthy they celebrate victory,
N ever beaten in the cup still victorious in luck,
D reaming of the World Cup training hard for Championship,
E very day they practise hard to win,
R eigning champions Castle Key.
L oving every minute of glee they celebrate victory,
A nd every year the players score about a million goals,
N ever falling, never dying,
D isaster falling to Division One, the players still are having fun.

James Baker (11)
Easington Colliery Primary School, Peterlee

Black Cats

Here comes the Black Cats,
Going to beat the Raggy Rats,
Here they are coming to play,
But the other team run away.
Here are the Magpies,
Looking smart in their ties,
Sitting down in their seats,
Does that mean they are neat?
The Black Cats kick the ball,
And the Magpies have a nasty fall,
The Magpies stand at the pole,
While the Black Cats score their goal.
Well that's the end of the game,
And the Magpies are a shame.
Because the Black Cats have won,
And that is how it's done!

Kassandra Starling (11)
Easington Colliery Primary School, Peterlee

Sunderland

On the big day,
The footballers play,
At the Stadium of Light,
They'll give up a fight.

As the players look out for the ball,
The mangers call,
Sunderland are hard,
But they might get a red card.

Sometimes it lasts till night,
But they still have all their might,
The supporters thought
That the ball was caught.

At the Stadium of Light,
They'll give up a fight.

Dannii Egan (10)
Easington Colliery Primary School, Peterlee

SAFC

Red and white army,
Black cats,
Red and white army,
Black cats.

99 years at Roker Park,
But now it's faded in the dark,
7 years at the Stadium of Light,
And, *wow,* what a wonderful sight.

Built on Wearmouth Colliery Ground,
Costing twenty million pounds,
49,000 seats it holds,
Everyone loves it really loads.

All our players must get a thrill,
Coming out of the tunnel to show us their skill,
Lots of excitement buzzing around,
In every part of the ground.

Our players are simply the best,
Leaving behind all the rest,
Mick McCarthy on the line,
Shouting instructions all the time.

Every game they try really hard,
Sometimes getting a yellow or red card,
That doesn't stop them giving up a fight,
Cos these are the boys from the
Stadium of Light.

James Connor (10)
Easington Colliery Primary School, Peterlee

Football Is My Life

F ootball is all that matters in my life
O pponents team is losing - hooray,
O ffside Woodgate,
T eam that wins is best,
B oots hanging from the lockers,
A rtificial lights keep the grass right,
' L ate one this match,' says Bobby Robson,
L ight shining around the Stadium.

S core is 6-1 to us,
T rophy is the biggest one ever,
A way game at Manchester,
D ream that I will be a professional one day,
I ndependent is what the referee is
U nderdogs are the losers,
M atch on the 2nd of March.

Lisa Surtees (10)
Easington Colliery Primary School, Peterlee

Stadium Of Light

One lovely day
Year 6 went on a trip,
To the Stadium of Light,
We had to go right round
The Stadium of Light,
I saw a cup that Sunderland won
We went in the classroom,
We did things about the Stadium of Light
And then on the seat above the badge.
Then we went to the PC room,
We played on the PC for a bit,
Then we went to the shop and got some things,
Then we got on the bus but it broke down ,
A different bus came and gave us a battery,
And then we went home.

Ryan Whittington (11)
Easington Colliery Primary School, Peterlee

I Went On A Trip

I went on a trip to the Stadium of Light,
Everyone was excited and as high as a kite,
As we sat on the bus Casey and me,
We looked out the window to see what we could see.

What Casey saw was a big delight,
We were here at the Stadium of Light,
The bus driver stopped and we got off the bus,
We both got wrong for making a fuss.

Casey so wanted to see the team,
She was screaming as if she was in a dream,
We ate our packed lunches and went on our way,
And before we knew it, it was the end of the day.

We got on the bus before Casey went to sleep,
She waved bye to the stadium and started to weep,
On the way back, we all sang a little song,
We were back in a min, it didn't take long.

I went on a trip to the Stadium of Light,
And when I came back it was near to night.

Katie Turner (10)
Easington Colliery Primary School, Peterlee

Our Trip

We went on a trip to the Stadium of Light,
When the bus broke down, it gave us a fright,
Another bus came to jump-start our bus,
We got home late but nobody made a fuss.

We went into the changing rooms,
We saw the shirts including Mart Pooms,
We had our lunch just past noon,
We were walking round the stadium soon.

I think that it is safe to say
We definitely enjoyed our day!

Claire Louise Smith (11)
Easington Colliery Primary School, Peterlee

Crazy Football

I love football, it is good,
I like football on the mud,
I love football on the yard,
I like football, it is hard.

Football is very sporty,
Sometimes the players are naughty,
They get into a big fight,
I wish I could, I just might.

I get ready to kick the ball,
One, two, three the phone call,
I wish I could play the team,
I wish I could, it's my dream.

Sunderland are the best,
They wear stripy vests,
They won the FA Cup
And jumped up.

Richard Creed (10)
Easington Colliery Primary School, Peterlee

Football Poem

Footballer is the best thing to be,
Off we go to Sunderland you see.
Onside is a good thing to be,
Training that's where the Sunderland team will be,
Bang goes the football in the goal,
Away the Sunderland team they go,
Like Sunderland they will dislike you.
Love Newcastle they will love you.
'Haway the lads' shout the Sunderland fans,
Every game they play, they lose,
Referee gives a red card,
Offside you are not supposed to be,
Sunderland is a bad team to support.

Daniel Simpson (10)
Easington Colliery Primary School, Peterlee

Newcastle United

N il-nil that's what we drew to Man Utd,
E ngland, Alan Shearer played for them,
W inning is Newcastle's best trick,
C orner which Robert sometimes takes,
A ccuna sometimes plays for them,
S hearer is our best goal scorer,
T rophies, Newcastle's got loads of them,
L avatory that's where fans go at half-time,
E xcellent! They've scored again! That's 5-0.

U nderdogs that's what the other teams are,
N orth stand that's where the away fans are,
I mpatient fans waiting to cause a riot,
T yneside is where the stadium is,
E ast stand is the greatest of them all,
D eath that's what happens in a riot.

Jordan Pegman (10)
Easington Colliery Primary School, Peterlee

My Visit

S underland's home ground - wow I'm here
T ricks and movements I learnt from the coach,
A way team disappointed by a score of 3-0,
D reams of the players to beat Newcastle 4-0,
I nside the changing room - look at those shirts,
U nder the tunnel, chilly breeze up my shirt,
M an Utd, sad and Sunderland happy.

O nly a win away,
F rom The Premiership.

L ights that shine high late at night,
I nside, the top left corner, shoot now!
G round so soft, so good to lie on,
H igh as a kite after the match,
T ooting the horn as we go past.

Jack Dunn (10)
Easington Colliery Primary School, Peterlee

The Stadium Of Light

Last Thursday I went to the Stadium of Light,
It was so big, I got quite a fright,
The players we did not meet,
But we got to sit in their seats.

We had a quiz
And I was a whiz,
We saw the Penshaw monument
Only for a few moments.

It was a learning through football day,
Even though we didn't get to play,
A certificate we all received,
To get outside we were all relieved.

When we got outside, we were cold,
We wouldn't see the bus till we were old,
When we got to school we were very late,
Someone brought keys to open the gate!

Sarah Barnes (10)
Easington Colliery Primary School, Peterlee

HaWay The Lads

H alf-time came,
A s the lads made the game.
W ait they scored a goal,
A aaa . . . it hit the pole!
Y ou could just say.

T he lads were crying,
H ow can they carry on?
E ventually they scored their goal.

L ucky it never hit the pole
A gain,
D idn't lose the game,
S uccess, they won, as the score was two.

Kathryn Bowley (11)
Easington Colliery Primary School, Peterlee

The Stadium Of Light

We went on a trip the other day,
We did not go too far away.

We sat in pairs upon the bus,
The teacher told us not to fuss.

We headed towards the Stadium of Light,
But not to watch a football fight.

We looked at the stadium in awe,
Then headed out to explore.

The away changing rooms get on my wick
And well and truly make me sick.

The seats on the football ground were very high,
It felt like you were in the sky.

We skidded around the footy pitch,
It's enough to give you a stitch.

What a wonderful day of delight,
The day we visited the Stadium of Light.

Rebecca Clymo (11)
Easington Colliery Primary School, Peterlee

Trip To The Stadium Of Light

Last week we went to the Stadium of Light,
Never saw the players and never saw them fight.

On the journey there it was quite a swizz,
Sophie Kenney had some pop with a bit of a fizz.

On the computer I saw a kite,
And the stadium's colour was red and white.

When we were buying at the shop,
We were looking at the prices, we were in a strop.

We saw these men, I'm sure they had pads,
But who cares, for them - Haway the lads!

Khyle Douglas Fryer (10)
Easington Colliery Primary School, Peterlee

The Stadium Of Light

We went to the Stadium of Light
On Thursday the 5th of February,
The sun was very, very bright
And we all thought it was great.

When we got into the stadium,
We had a little quiz
And we were in groups of four,
Some thought it was hard and
Some thought it was a whiz.

We went to look at the changing rooms
And my friend Sophie sat where Beckham sat,
The away changing rooms looked like a doom,
We all sat down for quite a bit.

We had 45 minutes to eat
And we sat with our partners,
We were all hot from the heaters,
We all eventually finished our lunch.

Joanna Maddison (10)
Easington Colliery Primary School, Peterlee

Stadium Of Light

I went to the Stadium of Light,
The weather was so bright.

We went into a classroom,
It was like a room of doom.

But we still had lots of fun
Shame we didn't dance around in the sun.

Then we had dinner,
Sunderland is a winner.

It was fun in the changing room,
I wish we were standing near Orlando Bloom.

Tasmin Johnson (11)
Easington Colliery Primary School, Peterlee

The School Trip

On Thursday the 5th of February
We went to the Stadium of Light.
The stadium was extraordinary
And the sun was shining bright.

At half-nine we got on the bus
To go on our school trip,
On the way there we passed Toys 'R' Us
In the window, a lucky dip.

When we got there, there was a front door,
With flowers all around,
Some people came down from the top floor,
Oh boy, I felt proud.

We went upstairs to the classroom
And took off our coats and bags,
I saw a good picture of Mart Poom
And of the rest of the lads.

We went downstairs to the changing rooms
And learnt about Sunderland FC,
The away room with greens and blues
To make them sick you see.

We went outside and sat on the badge
Oh what a good sight we saw,
We all shouted 'Haway the lads'
But it sounded like a roar.

We went back to get our bags
And coats to get ready to set off home
We all said 'Thank you lads'
And that is the end of my poem.

David Griffiths (11)
Easington Colliery Primary School, Peterlee

Trip To The Stadium Of Light

Our school went to the Stadium of Light,
It really was quite big,
We went upstairs to sit on the badge,
Sweat was on my brow,
I got to put on Mick McCarthy's T-shirt,
He is the manager, you know,
We got to see 'Haway the lads,'
But I got to shout it out loud,
We went in the changing rooms,
I sat in a foreign guy's seat,
I can't remember his name.
We went in the gift shop,
Just got three pencil sharpeners,
When we came out of the gift shop
The bus broke down,
Finally we got back to school
Late!
That was the trip to the Stadium of Light,
A day I'll never forget.

Philip Milburn (11)
Easington Colliery Primary School, Peterlee

The Stadium Of Light

On Thursday we went to
The Stadium of Light,
We saw the changing rooms,
It was red and white.

It had 'Ha'way the lads,'
On the seats,
And we saw the commentary box,
Where Gary Lineker sits.

Sophie sat where Beckham sat,
She didn't even know,
We went in a classroom,
And did a little quiz.

Patrick Bonnar (10)
Easington Colliery Primary School, Peterlee

On The Bus To The Trip

We're all going to the Stadium of Light,
Most of us had been up all night,
As we turned the corner we could see the place,
That put a smile on our face.

As we get off the bus,
The teachers shout - oh what a fuss!
We all enjoyed the stadium
But we had a shock in store for us.

The bus had broken down,
Our smiles turned into frowns,
We waited until three,
We were very unhappy you see.

When we got home,
Our hair needed a comb,
Because we were blown away,
Waiting for the bus.

Stephanie Louise Bell (11)
Easington Colliery Primary School, Peterlee

Me And My Friends At The Stadium Of Light

I remember waking up and thinking,
'Will I have a good time with my mates?'

I will tell you one thing,
It was class.
Me and my mass of friends
Won a badge and there
Was nothing to hide.

I felt me and my team had pride,
We wore the Sunderland tops,
I felt as proud as a cop.

It was cool and it
Could not have been cooler.

Jack Mather (11)
Easington Colliery Primary School, Peterlee

The Trip

This is my poem
This is my rhyme
I'm writing about Sunderland
Writing a couple of lines.

The sun was shining
It was shining bright
It was just the right time
To go to the Stadium of Light.

'Haway the lads' we shouted into the crowd,
It echoed like thunder and it was quite loud,
At half-past twelve, we had our lunch,
We went to the toilet and came back for more of a munch.

At 3 o'clock the bus broke down
And we were stuck in the middle of Sunderland town.

So this is my poem
This is my rhyme
I was writing about Sunderland
Writing a couple of lines.

Anthony Jackson (10)
Easington Colliery Primary School, Peterlee

Our School Trip Of Stadium

The Stadium of Light
Was quite a fright.

Everybody went to the shop
Some people bought some pop.

Everyone shouted 'Haway the lads,'
Footballers wear their pads.

On the way to Sunderland
Some of us saw Matalan.

Sophie K was sitting in David Beckham's seat,
Some of were eating meat.

We saw Toys 'R' Us
Our bus broke down and then another one came.

Adelle Bailey (11)
Easington Colliery Primary School, Peterlee

The Winter Sky

The sky at night is beautiful
With stars as white as snow
The colour of the sky, a dark, velvet blue
The moon like a cat's claw
A crescent sliver of ice.

Abbie Hartley (10)
Hylton Red House Primary School, Sunderland

Peace Prayer

Can one man do it
Or maybe two
Or all of Britain's gallant few?
Whether it be sunshine
Whether it be rain,
Bless all our soldiers in so much pain
And bless poor children out there in Iraq
Who want their life and family back.

Louise Kelly (11)
Hylton Red House Primary School, Sunderland

Alien

Little alien from outer space,
With a glowing green-glass face,
Huge saucer eyes shining bright,
Rival the moon and starlight.

Tiny legs, four inches tall,
Big round feet just like a ball,
Pointed ears, a devil's tail,
From a cold planet of snow and hail.

Luke Matthews (10)
Hylton Red House Primary School, Sunderland

Harry Potter

My name is Harry Potter
And I go to Hogwarts School,
Whenever I go there,
I act so very cool,
My days are so exciting,
Magic spells and a flying broom,
And when night comes, I go off to bed,
If the stars let me reach my room.

Barry Small (11)
Hylton Red House Primary School, Sunderland

Lives

Some people have nothing,
Some people do,
Theirs are lives you can do nothing to.

Nothing to eat,
Nowhere to sleep,
Living alone,
No one to phone.

No family or friends,
Their suffering never ends,
People waiting for their lives to end.

Faye Richardson (11)
Hylton Red House Primary School, Sunderland

Why?

Why is there brightness in the sky?
Why do people have to die?
Why is the grass the colour green?
Why are bullies always mean?

Why do people buy with money?
Why do bees always make honey?
Why do birds fly in the sky?
If you know, please tell me why.

Samantha Jones (11)
Hylton Red House Primary School, Sunderland

Weather!

The moon hides behind a cloud,
The thunder screams loudly,
The rain stamps its feet,
The wind ruffles my hair,
The lightning draws a Z in the sky.

Amy King (11)
Hylton Red House Primary School, Sunderland

Winter Nights

W is for winter
 I is for the icy cold breeze
N is for the night
T is for the leafless trees
E is for the very early morning
R is for the shiny ring around the moon.

N is for the cold winter's night
 I is for the ice on the ground
G is for glistening moon
H is for the hibernating animals
T is for the snowy trees
S is for the sun rising in the morning.

Sara Hodgson (11)
Hylton Red House Primary School, Sunderland

Heard It In Maths Class

Heard it in maths class
Heard it in maths class
'Give me my sheet'
'Stop trying to cheat'
Heard it in maths class
'Give me my book'
'Stop picking on Luke'
Heard it in maths class
Heard it in maths class
'Be quiet, it's a test'
'Just because I'm the best'
Heard it in maths class
Heard it in maths class
Talking to you!

Nathan Gaffney (11)
John F Kennedy Primary School, Washington

Tell Me What It Is

There's something in my bedroom,
I don't know what it is,
It lurks around my window,
So tell me what it is.

It hides behind the curtain,
And behind the cupboard door,
It walks across my desk,
I can see it on my floor.

There's something in my cupboard,
It's chewing all my clothes,
I can see it walking on my bed,
It's biting at my toes.

There's something creeping under my bed,
It's shadows on my wall,
It's creeping around my door,
It's playing with my ball.

I'm getting up right now,
To find out what it is,
I'm putting on the light,
It's only my cat Riz.

Laura Thompson (10)
John F Kennedy Primary School, Washington

World

W hy are you destroying the trees around me?
O nly a few animals are going to survive.
R uining our wildlife, it is a shame.
L eave our world alone.
D ying animals are soon going to be extinct!

Rebecca Oliver (8)
John F Kennedy Primary School, Washington

In A School Kitchen

There are fleas in the kitchen
The boys are always itching
The ladies say, 'Eat your food'
But watch out, they might get in a mood

There's mud all around
So don't sit on the ground
Their soup is so bad
That they go mad

The sink is full of plates
That they come out the kitchen gates
The cupboards are full of spiders
That they seem like minders

The benches break
That nobody likes to take
The pipes are bare
That nobody cares

And that's what a school kitchen's like.

Abby Spalding (9)
John F Kennedy Primary School, Washington

How My Budgie Squawked

My budgie squawked all day
My budgie squawked all night
But when I walked into the room
My budgie got a fright

My budgie is so small
Smaller than three blind mice
Whenever I walked into the room
My budgie squawked twice.

Christina Baird (10)
John F Kennedy Primary School, Washington

The Dumb Cheerleader In My School

The dumb cheerleader in my school
She's dumb and acts like a fool
She waves her pom poms in the air
And flicks her shiny blonde hair.

I told her once that's not enough
She acts as though she's really tough
When she gets home
She gets out her comb.

She fancies all the popular guys
And they love the twinkle in her eyes
She thought she was so good
With her confidence you surely would.

The dumb cheerleader in my school
She's dumb and acts like a fool
She waves her pom poms in the air
And flicks her shiny blonde hair.

She's so not cool.

Lauren Ryan (11)
John F Kennedy Primary School, Washington

My Teacher Said

My teacher said I make no sense
So when I enter a competition
It makes me really tense.

But one day I wrote this poem
When I'd finished I thought, *that'll show 'em*
I sent my poem to the editors of the book
When I got a copy, I shouted, 'Look, look, look!'

My teacher shouted out loud
'I am so proud!'

Emily Moralee (10)
John F Kennedy Primary School, Washington

Beggar

Unloved and lonely,
Cold and wet,
Sad and hurt,
No money he met.

It happened one time,
In broad moonlight,
He was told to be gone,
It was a terrible sight.

A pain began late that night,
Within his broken heart,
Then the weather caught him,
Ripped his rags apart.

Children always kicked him,
People said he smelled,
But he lay there quietly,
Looking at the food they held.

I was watching from a bridge,
I saw him lying there,
I watched people go past,
Sniggering without a care.

Unloved and lonely,
Cold and wet,
Sad and hurt,
No money he met.

Claire Savage (11)
John F Kennedy Primary School, Washington

A Trip To The Supermarket

My grandma took a trip to the supermarket and brought some . . .
Apples and
Bananas and
Carrots and
Dairy Milk and
Eggs and
Flavourings and
Gammon and
Hash browns and
Ice lollies and
Jelly and
Kiwi fruit and
Lemons and
Melons and
Nuts and
Oranges and
Peppers and
Qcumber and
Ugly fruit and
Vanilla ice cream and
Watermelon and
Xtra large fizzy pop and
Yoghurt and
Zzzzz . . .
   'Grandma, I think we need a bigger basket.'

Ben Williams (11)
John F Kennedy Primary School, Washington

The History Daydreamer

History, history, history,
History, history, history . . .
Makes me daydream,

Queen Victoria, the Victorian Queen
Henry VIII, the fat king starting his reign in 1509,
Hera the goddess of all gods,

Or . . .
Cleopatra's servant getting fed to the snakes,
An ancient Greek pottery maker,
A caveman lighting a fire,

Anyway . . .
Who shot John F Kennedy?
Who shot his killer?
But the killer's killer died mysteriously,
But the killer's killer died mysteriously?
But the killer's killer died mysteriously?

'Rebecca!' the teacher cries,
I jump out of my skin,
The next history lesson awaits!

Rebecca Pike (11)
John F Kennedy Primary School, Washington

Animals

As extinct as an elephant
As killed as a kangaroo
As destroyed as a duck
As dead as a dolphin
As terrified as a turtle
As wiped out as a wolf
As frightened as a fox
As scared as a sea lion.

Alex Jenkins (7)
John F Kennedy Primary School, Washington

Grandma's Birthday

I'll tell you a story
It happened just the other day
It's all about a party
In a happy sort of way.

A party for my grandma
She's 70 years old
Drinking fine sherry
A happy old soul.

The music blaring
My mum dancing in a crowd
Waving her hands
Fooling around.

Too much to drink
More than enough
That's what it'll be
I'll have to get tough.

So when you're drinking
Just remember my mum
Waving her hands
Just like a clown.

Sophie Hylands (10)
John F Kennedy Primary School, Washington

Wonderful World

A tree is going to die. With all its might it tries to stay alive.
N ature is fighting with all its might.
 I n its branches all kinds of creatures make their homes.
M ore and more animals rush away from the trees, as they
                                                            crash to the earth.
A nimals without a home.
L ong, hard time in a rainforest staying alive.

Kenny Robson (7)
John F Kennedy Primary School, Washington

My Zoo

I wish I had a monkey,
It would swing me round the trees.
I wish I had a tiger
To scare away the bees.
I wish I had a giraffe
So I could climb upon its neck.
I wish I had a dolphin,
We could explore a deep, dark wreck.
I wish I had a zebra,
It could take me to the park.
I wish I had a cat
So it could guide me through the dark.
I wish I had a penguin
It could help me across the ice.
I wish I had an elephant
That isn't afraid of mice.
So if I wish and wish some more
My wish might actually come true,
Then I'd collect my animals
And open up my zoo!

Shorna Liddle (11)
John F Kennedy Primary School, Washington

My Mam

My mam is really cool
But when she goes out she sometimes acts like a fool
Once she has had a drink or two she falls down to the ground
When she gets off the ground she asks for another round
When she is finally in her house
She shuts her eyes, quiet as a mouse
The next day when she opened one eye
She gets a pain in her head and it looks like she is going to cry

'I'll never have another drink
Until next week is what I think.'

Emma Donnison (11)
John F Kennedy Primary School, Washington

Why Do I Hate The Way I Look

Why do I hate the way I look?
Maybe because my head is such a size.
Why do I hate the way I look?
Maybe because it's my funny, strange eyes.

Why do I hate the way I look?
Maybe because it's my big fat belly.
Why do I hate the way I look?
Maybe because my socks are so smelly.

Why do I hate the way I look?
Maybe because it's my hippy hips.
Why do I hate the way I look?
Maybe because it's my small, juicy lips.

Why do I hate the way I look?
Maybe because it's my long, hairy legs.
Why do I hate the way I look?
Maybe because it's my sumo kegs.

Why do I hate the way I look?
Maybe because it's my big, skinny neck.
Why do I hate the way I look?
Maybe because who cares, what the heck!

Rebecca Foster (10)
John F Kennedy Primary School, Washington

Would You

Would you cry if someone pushed you over?
Would you tell someone?
Would you let someone from the street into your home?
Would you let them stay out in the rain?

Would you be racist?
Would you be friends with a black person?
Would you do something you know is wrong?
Would you tell a teacher if you knew that someone was going
                                        to do something bad?

Jamie Hunter (10)
John F Kennedy Primary School, Washington

What Shall I Do?

What shall I do?
I haven't got a clue!
I don't know why,
But I just can't think!
What on earth shall I do?

I could call on my friends?
But they're all out!
I could ask my mum,
But she's no fun!
I don't know what to do,
I really don't!

Well I know what to do!
I will ask my dad what to do!
I'll go downstairs and see what he thinks!

'Dad, what shall I do?'
'What shall you do?
'I know what you will do
Do your homework.'
Well, it's not very good
But at least I've got something to do!

Hanna Lamb (10)
John F Kennedy Primary School, Washington

Wonderful Wildlife

A ll the animals in the world are being destroyed.
N ot all the animals are alive now.
I n the swampy forests, people are cutting down the trees.
M ammals are being destroyed as well.
A ll the animals are hurt and dying very quickly.
L ots of the tigers and lions are being destroyed.

Estelle Stephenson (7)
John F Kennedy Primary School, Washington

The Space Monster

I went off in my spacecraft,
I got caught up in space,
Then I saw a space monster,
Walk up to his base.

The monster had some colours,
Blue, red, purple and green,
He showed me all his brothers,
Do you want to be on our team?

He asked me a question,
'Where are all the stars?'
I answered him back to that,
'They're on top of Mars.'

He told me all about himself,
His age was twenty-five,
He then told me about his family,
All they want to do is stay alive.

The space monster was my friend,
He was a bit like a man,
We went on Mars and looked about,
And then saw a rolling can.

Liam Foster (8)
John F Kennedy Primary School, Washington

Wildlife

W hen will we stop destroying the earth?
 I n some places, animals can't give birth.
 L eaving animals there on the ground to die.
 D estroying the ozone layer in the sky.
 L ions and tigers are becoming rare.
 I n England there are hardly any wildlife there.
 F inding deer bones on the ground,
 E ven where animals can't be found.

Garry Cooper (8)
John F Kennedy Primary School, Washington

Hiding

He was hiding in the house,
He was as quiet as a mouse.

He wouldn't sit down,
He wouldn't care if someone was about to drown.

He moved to the corner,
But missed the sauna.

He went downstairs,
But didn't see any bears.

He went in the kitchen,
Quick, the dogs were itching.

He went for a cake,
Which his mam's just baked.

And it's in his tummy!

John Metcalfe (9)
John F Kennedy Primary School, Washington

Angel

There once was a girl I knew,
Who spread her wings and flew,
But I did not know,
That she was quite so-so.

There once was a girl I knew,
And because the sea was blue,
She shut her wings and fell,
Into a giant oyster shell.

There once was a girl I knew,
Who spread her wings and flew,
She was really quite peculiar,
Because she was an angel.

Jenni McDermott (9)
John F Kennedy Primary School, Washington

Bullied

She stands in her room
Looking so sad
'Cause she's getting bullied
By this lad.

She walks through the gate
Looking so weepy
'Cause she's getting bullied
That she's still sleepy.

She walks to the door
With a terrible fright
'Cause she's getting bullied
That can't be right.

She sits in the classroom
She can't change places
'Cause she's getting bullied
This lad's pulling faces.

Is this girl you or
Are you just a bully *too*?

Chelsea Hourigan (10)
John F Kennedy Primary School, Washington

Wildlife

W e are destroying and changing our Earth,
 I n no time at all we'll celebrate no birth.
 L ooking out my window I can see so many hopeless things,
 D on't leave our world looking like this, I don't hear many
                                                    birds that sing.
 L ook all around you, what have we done?
 I n all different countries, there's no hope for some!
 F or here in the rainforest, the wildlife have no homes or food.
 E veryone please help, put me in a good mood!

Charlotte Casey (8)
John F Kennedy Primary School, Washington

The Ting Tong Tree

The ting tong tree is very scary
So little kids you better be wary
The ting tong tree is a wonderful thing
It can make you laugh, it can make you sing
The ting tong tree has its ups and downs
Like last week it ate a clown
The ting tong tree is really wild
Last week it kicked a child

The ting tong tree is brown
He always has a constant frown
The ting tong tree can bellow
He hates the colour yellow
The ting tong tree is very scary
So little kids you better be wary!

Johnathon Cobain (10)
John F Kennedy Primary School, Washington

Animal Show

I saw an animal show
Where there were animals spread out across the floor.
A man came out from behind a curtain,
And brought a stick, of that I was certain.

The evil man produced a whip,
While the seconds continued to tick.
I looked at the animals, I couldn't bear,
And soon I got out of my chair.
I went to the man and grabbed his whip,
I said, 'Can I just give you a tip?'

Smack!

Jade Langley (10)
John F Kennedy Primary School, Washington

Why!

I'm just going to get a sledgehammer.
Why?
Because I need to knock the wall down.
Why?
Because it's infested with spiders.
Why?
Because spiders like walls.
Why?
Because they're dark inside.
Why?
If you don't stop shouting why at me I'll knock you down with it.
Why?
Aaarrrggghhh!
Why?

Jamie Kelly (11)
John F Kennedy Primary School, Washington

Animals In Danger

R are animals are starting to die.
A nimals were living fair and square but now they're all dying.
I n the world animals are dying because of the people who
                                        cut down the rainforests.
N arrow tigers can quickly and fastly eat you.
F orests aren't important to people but forests are important
                                                to animals
O nly a few animals left in the world we live in.
R ats are dying out because of us and because of workmen.
E lephants are dying too because of the world we live in.
S nakes are dying because of us. One day
T igers will leap up high, but know they're dying.

Nicola Hawkins (7)
John F Kennedy Primary School, Washington

Here Comes

Here comes Monday
School has begun day
It's a hit and run day
There goes Monday

Here comes Tuesday
It is a blues day
Then it's brighten up day
There goes Tuesday

Here comes Wednesday
It is a fear day
The bully pulls ears day
There goes Wednesday

Here comes Thursday
We go swimming day
It is time for choir day
There goes Thursday

Here comes Friday
I eat pies day
It's TV day
There goes Friday.

David Grist (9)
John F Kennedy Primary School, Washington

Wildlife

W hen I was young, this place was green, but now I've grown.
 I have noticed more and more changes.
L ots of animals I have seen have disappeared.
D oesn't anyone see that things are changing?
L ife has gone, trees are dying.
 I n our world around us we are creating an enormous mess.
F ew animals are going to survive.
E veryone will soon be dead, what should we do about it?

Alexandra Heather Mitchell (7)
John F Kennedy Primary School, Washington

Here Comes . . .

Here comes Monday,
School has begun day,
It's a hit and run day,
There goes Monday.

Here comes Tuesday,
It's my birthday,
Gonna have a fun day,
Hurrah for Tuesday.

Here comes Wednesday,
Middle of the week day,
Our PE day,
There goes Wednesday.

Here comes Thursday,
It's a swimming day,
It's a wet hair day,
We like Thursday.

Here comes Friday,
Last day of school day,
Going on holiday,
Yippee for Friday.

Ashley Stone (9)
John F Kennedy Primary School, Washington

Wildlife

W ho threw the rubbish in the lake?
  I can look after animals
  L eopards stare through your window
  D ogs lie on the ground
  L ions roar like a forest
  I can sing like a bird
  F riendly animals may be friends but may have to die
  E lephants will be dying with no food.

Kate Robson (7)
John F Kennedy Primary School, Washington

Letters Down

A n excellent ant lives in ground.

P erfect queen is beautiful sitting on a throne.
O xygen is air but you can't see it.
E lement is green jewel,
M onsters climbing around.

I is for ice cube, a cube that freezes.
S is for snow, it is beautiful and white.

F is for fun going on rides.
U is for umbrella when it rains.
N is for netball for playing a game.

F is for food, for eating food.
O is for open, for opening a door.
R is for running, always running.

E is for elephant, it was drinking water.
V is for violin, it plays a sweet song.
E is for eagle, it crosses the skies.
R is for red, it's a colour.
Y is for yacht, it is a boat in sailing.
O is for opposite, to face each other.
N is for negative, a number is negative.
E is for evaporation, it's part of science.

Donna Cowie (10)
John F Kennedy Primary School, Washington

Wildlife

A nimals need one more chance
N o one can hear their cries
I should help all the animals
M ammals and babies should have more trees
A ll the animals are dying because of us
L eave them alone.

William Brightman (7)
John F Kennedy Primary School, Washington

You Don't Frighten Me!

When I get frightened . . .

I stack,
I pack,
I pile,
I file
All my teddies around my bed
And like soldiers at attention
They offer me a wall of protection.

Then I skip into my bed,
Squeeze deep down into my duvet and whisper,
'Come on darkness,
You big, black bullying
Bubble of trouble.
I'm ready with my teddies
And getting ready to beat you up,
So come out, come out wherever you are
And you don't frighten me!'

Jade Ferguson (9)
John F Kennedy Primary School, Washington

Extinct

Elephants are stampeding and crying!
X means stop! Everything dying.
The beautiful forest is getting destroyed!
In a rainforest there is a riot.
Crying snakes and crying cheetahs
Kingfishers are dying to meet us
End of animals and lovely trees
Dying creatures, help them please.

Jack Spalding (7)
John F Kennedy Primary School, Washington

My Cat Millie

My cat Millie,
She is so fun,
And very funny,
I play with her a ton.

She is black and white,
So funny and cute,
She'd probably chase a kite,
She would sniff my boot.

She is an indoor cat,
But runs fast,
Millie certainly is not fat,
Plus in a race she'd not be last.

Millie has sharp claws,
She usually fights with me,
But has soft paws,
She doesn't listen to a rattling key.

Courtney Ross (9)
John F Kennedy Primary School, Washington

Animals

E lephants are getting hurt.
X is stop lots of trees getting chopped down.
T rees are getting chopped down like my friend's oak trees.
I saw all of my best friends getting brown.
N ut trees, I saw them getting chopped down.
C ompost, I had soil under me. Elephants are going for a drink
in the clean water.

T orching the forest.

Jack Dodds (8)
John F Kennedy Primary School, Washington

The Fantastic Beast

One fantastic beast,
He likes to have a human feast,
With his red, blotchy eyes,
In the shadow of the dark skies.

He lurks around,
Making no sound,
With claws that can nip,
And uses his tail as a whip.

When he uses his tail,
It's every time you look at it you'll go pale,
He'll take you away,
You couldn't even say I want to stay.

He'll eat you up full,
In his dark cave that is extremely dull,
You could shout, 'He's going to kill me!'
But no one would come up to be his tea.

Kate Wilkins (10)
John F Kennedy Primary School, Washington

Animal World

As happy as a kangaroo
As excited as an elephant
As furry as a monkey
As fussy as a parrot
As fat as a pig
As cross as a bull
As sneaky as a leopard
As slimy as a snake.

Tasha Bradbury (7)
John F Kennedy Primary School, Washington

My Mam, Your Mam

My mam's taller than your mam.
Yes, but Mam's taller than you,
If she gets any taller she won't fit in the house,
She'll have to live outdoors.

Yes, but my mam's smells more than your mam.
My mam smells OK,
She's only got two socks left
And they're both going green and slimy.

Ah, but Mam's fatter than your mam,
My mam's fatter, all right.
She can't sit in the Grand Canyon,
She'll have to live in space.

Yes, but my mam's smarter than your mam,
My mam is smarter alright.
She is smarter than a calculator
And I am sick of her.

But my mam is friends with your mam,
Mine's friends with yours too.
I think they don't like us,
But we don't like them too.

Reece Young (11)
John F Kennedy Primary School, Washington

Animal

A tree is getting hurt, a feeling it's going to die!
N o people will hurt but a tree is going to cry.
 I n my world many years ago there were green leaves in the sky.
M y world now is becoming too hot, no one is going to live.
A s the world has gone too far, no one is going to give.
 L et's help the world, let's have hope.

Rachael Turnbull (7)
John F Kennedy Primary School, Washington

The Hand

This is the hand
that took the axe
that chopped the wood
and killed the tree.

This is the hand
that cut the bread
that made the sandwich
and gave it to me.

This is the hand
that rubbed the sticks
that made the fire
and kept me warm.

This is the hand
on the cold water tap
that poured me a drink
and kept me cool.

This is the hand
that poured the drink
that made the fire
that made the sandwich
that chopped the wood.
This is the hand
that knows what to do.

Adam Dawson (11)
John F Kennedy Primary School, Washington

Stop Animals In Danger

H ope for the animals that they don't die,
O nly a few trees survive,
P lease don't spoil our environment,
E xplore the world and let animals run free.

Sophie Danskin (8)
John F Kennedy Primary School, Washington

The Space Monster

The space monster's colour
Was as blue as the sea,
He smelt like smelly socks
And the smell affected me!

The space monster's eyes
Were as sharp as a blade of grass,
He had messy purple hair
And ate extremely rusty copper and brass!

The space monster's eyebrows
Were as creamy as banana-yellow,
His back was as pink as a pig,
From that angle he looked like a marshmallow.

The space monster's teeth
Needed a big clean,
They were slimy and orange
And his hand was where his ear should have been!

The space monster began
To get ready to go,
But before he went he began to shoot!
And I had to duck down low!

Nasim Asl (9)
John F Kennedy Primary School, Washington

Wonderful Animals

A rhinoceros is so rare, it will soon die out.
N earby is a jungle, the elephants are dying right now.
I am so, so sad, if any more die there will be none left.
M ammals are dying out because people throw rubbish
in the fresh sea.
A ll the tigers are terrified, their homes are getting chopped down.
L et's share our lush world and treat it like we care.

Sarah Cobain (7)
John F Kennedy Primary School, Washington

Stop It!

Stop picking your nose
Stop chewing your toes
Stop cracking your fingers
Stop calling your sisters mingers
Stop jumping from the top stair
Stop rocking on your chair
Stop showing us your tum
Stop sucking your thumb
Stop kissing the girls
Stop pulling their curls
Stop drawing on your hands
Stop flicking rubber bands
Stop eating modelling clay . . .
. . . Why do dads act this way?

Natalie Brown (11)
John F Kennedy Primary School, Washington

Why?

Mam, shall I feed the cats?
    Why?
Because it's my turn to feed them.
    Why?
Because it's Monday.
    Why?
Because God made it Monday.
    Why?
Because he wanted to.
    Why?
Because that's what he wanted.
    Why?
Will you ever stop saying why?
    Why?
Go to the shop, get some cat food and feed the cats.
    What?

Nicola Freckleton (11)
John F Kennedy Primary School, Washington

Why Is She?

Why is she coming home crying?
Why is she not eating?
Maybe she's hurt herself
And she can't be bothered?

Why is she not talking to us?
Why is she walking to school with her head down?
Maybe she's broken up with her friends
And can't make up again?

Why is she not working?
Why is she always getting crosses on her work?
Maybe she's just upset
And just wants to sort it out herself?

I need to know why
Otherwise it's going to get worse.

Emma Scott (10)
John F Kennedy Primary School, Washington

Do You Think?

Do you think fish can fly?
Do you think birds can cry?

Do you think eels can talk?
Do you think snowmen can walk?

Do you think Santa will come in July?
Do you think ghosts can die?

Do you think pies can jump?
Do you think camels have a hump?

Do you think?

Kimberley Coulter (9)
John F Kennedy Primary School, Washington

School's Funny!

Dominic's tripped over an apple peel,
and Tim is pulling the teacher's sticky seal,
and Jan is waiting for her meal.

Ian is picking his nose
and Sharney's doing a pose
and Keiran is showing off his new clothes.

Karl is messing the computers
and David is using a hooter
and Jack is going down the corridors on a scooter.

Connolly is dancing so far
that Daniel is seeing stars
and Kate has nicked Mrs Looter's car.

John is flapping his cape about
and Johnny has kicked his football far out
and, by accident, the plumber has broken the spout.

Rebecca is finishing her maths,
and Mrs Looter slipped into the swimming baths,
and Roy has failed his SATs.

Now Sarah is looking and she'll see,
Anna has made a mess of her literacy
it wouldn't be good for you and me!

Luke is saying to Pat, *'Stop it!'*
and Mr Davidson is calling Michael a muppet
and Steve is saying to Ben, 'Let's do it!'

The class is doing PE
but Dom's desperate for a wee
and Liam has really banged his knee - ouch!

And now is the end of 'School's Funny'
and remember, in school, don't be a bully!

Michael Grist (9)
John F Kennedy Primary School, Washington

Under The Sea

Under the sea it is dark,
Under the sea you find sharks,
Under the sea the fish swim,
Under the sea the whales are dim,
Under the sea the shells are scared.

Under the sea the cod play,
Under the sea the coley say,
Under the sea the seaweed swing,
Under the sea the mackerel sing,
Under the sea the shrimps dance.

Under the sea the flatfish jump,
Under the sea the seals thump,
Under the sea the dogfish see,
Under the sea the sole fish moves,
Under the sea the fish swim free.

James Thompson (11)
John F Kennedy Primary School, Washington

My Day At School

At my school,
I get no attention,
Sometimes I'm having detention.

At dinner time,
Everyone acts like they have the *flea!*
Sometimes they even have a *wee!*

At PE
My friends speak in rhyme,
Sometimes I feel I did a crime.

At home time,
It's poem time.

Goodbye!
Poem rhyme.

Naomi Andersson (8)
John F Kennedy Primary School, Washington

Feelings Beyond

When someone feels sad
You might feel bad,
They might go and cry,
They might wish they would die,
When you've made someone frown
You might feel like a clown.

When someone feels down
They might give you a frown,
Some people are worried
Because they're being bullied.
If you say goodbye
Someone might cry.

Sometimes you wonder why
Some people cry,
Some people feel alone
When they're on their own,
What if you feel sad
But they feel bad.

Sometimes I wonder
Why people feel under,
If someone's in need
Then do a good deed,
You might need a friend,
Someone to depend.

Sheryl Hedley (9)
John F Kennedy Primary School, Washington

Dragon

D ragon, dragon, don't be afraid
R ide up high into the sky
A hhh! That's too high!
G oing to China, it is fun
O n a plane to the rising sun
N ow I say goodbye. Hope you have fun in China.

Christopher Barton (8)
John F Kennedy Primary School, Washington

My Little Angel Star

My angel came to me one night,
Her wings glowing so, so bright,
Her gentle touch is all I need,
She is the water and I am the seed.

She cares for me in all I do,
She could do wonders for you too,
With her I do everything right,
Until one day she takes into flight.

My angel's gone forever now,
All I have left of her is her little toy cow,
I watch the stars every night,
Wishing she was here with me,
Shining evermore bright.

Shannan Mullen (9)
John F Kennedy Primary School, Washington

Stop, Full Stop

She goes to school
Crying like a fool,
She's not a bad girl,
Her name is pearl.

The boys and girls pick on her
Just because she wears fur,
They always make her hurl,
Then they make her twirl.

Why does she come home weeping?
Then she's sleeping,
She never starts eating,
Why is she doing secret keeping?

  The secret is
  She's getting
  Bullied,
    Stop, full stop.

Megan Laing (9)
John F Kennedy Primary School, Washington

I Want This

I want a skateboard,
I want a computer,
I want some sweets,
I want a pet,
Now.

I want to go to a theme park,
I want to go to America,
I want a car,
I want a computer game,
Now.

I want a mansion,
I want a motorbike,
I want some toys,
I want a swimming pool,
I want everything,
Now.

I want never gets.

Benjamin Butterfield (11)
John F Kennedy Primary School, Washington

Who?

Who put the colour in the rainbow?
Who made the colourful play dough?
Who made the gooey clay?
Who let us play?

Who made horrible school?
Who invented the swimming pool?
Who made my giggly laugh?
Who invented the complicated graph?

Who made us very good?
Who gave us all the food?
Who gave us all of these?
Can you tell me please?

Hannah Wylie (9)
John F Kennedy Primary School, Washington

Space Monster

I woke up all of a sudden,
I heard a funny sound,
I went to the window,
And this is what I found.

A creamy-green monster,
Standing and very much alive,
His eyes as blue as the sea,
His teeth as sharp as knives.

All of a sudden,
He asked me to dance,
But I said no,
So he tried to eat me.

I got that scared,
I had to run down France,
With the alien behind *me!*

Kelsey Duncan (8)
John F Kennedy Primary School, Washington

Swan

The white winged angel,
Floating bright,
I stare at it,
An amazing sight.

Its legs are spread,
Its eyes are wide,
Preparing softly,
For its glide.

The body is white,
Sleek and slender,
Gazing at me,
Very tender.

Philippa Ogden (10)
John F Kennedy Primary School, Washington

I Know I Saw A Monster

I know I saw a monster,
It came out of my bed,
It came down to attack me,
Just after I'd been fed.

I know I saw a monster,
His eyes were big and blue,
He was as smelly as a skunk,
Oh whatever shall I do?

I know I saw a monster,
His hair was spiky and pink,
He looked like he was stupid,
So let's think, think, think.

I know I saw a monster,
And it gave a mighty roar,
I just stayed in my spot and said,
'Come on, let's hear more.'

I know I saw a monster,
So I picked up a sword,
But straight after he died,
I realised I was bored.

Michael Watkis (9)
John F Kennedy Primary School, Washington

Girls' Power

G is for girly girl
I is for interesting clothes
R is for rich girls that get everything
L is for London, the beautiful sights of a girl's face
S is for so beautiful, just like all of the girls
   This is for all of the girls in the world.

Stephanie Ellwood (9)
John F Kennedy Primary School, Washington

Why?

I'm just going out for a moment.
Why?
To make a drink.
Why?
Because I'm thirsty.
Why?
I have a dry throat.
Why?
Because it's a dry day.
Why?
Because it is.
Why?
Just shut up.
What!

Stacey Harris (10)
John F Kennedy Primary School, Washington

Paintings

After school all the paintings we have done
come out to play and have some fun.
This must be why, yesterday, when we came in
it looked like someone had committed an awful sin.
The paintings had trashed all the school
you would think there had been a ghoul.
Someone in reception had painted a teddy bear
someone in Year 1 had painted a picture now with a tear.
Someone in Year 2 had painted a lollipop
someone in Year 3 had painted the big top.
Someone in Year 4 had painted a clock saying tick tock
someone in Year 5 had painted a sock.
And that's why Year 6 are simply the best
we were practising for our test!

Jenny Cawson (10)
John F Kennedy Primary School, Washington

An Alien

The alien was as round as a pea
The alien was blue as the sea
His name was Sloppy as can be
He ate all bees and fleas.

Sloppy was the worst animal you'd ever seen.
He looked like jelly and a fuzzy bee
He was really spotty like he had chickenpox
And he was going to turn into a bee.

His hair was spiky as can be
His hair was fuzzy hair that didn't match me
Because he looked like a tree
And he had a best mate called Lee.

They came up to me and really scared me
They had a big spaceship as big as a tree
I went over to the spaceship and this is what happened
Bang! Straight at my knee.

Danielle Roberts (9)
John F Kennedy Primary School, Washington

Arguments

I'm sitting in my garden, cold and all alone.
I really want to go back in but I feel it's not my home.
My mam raised her hands to me, I cried with all my tears.
I don't want to go back in, I'm so full of fear.

I really want to go back in and sleep the whole night through
And wake up in a dreamland somewhere nice with you.
But now it's all sorted, I love my mam so true.
I think she does the same but I still like to come and see you.

Sarah Bradley (10)
John F Kennedy Primary School, Washington

The Monster

The monster was as tall as a rocket
He was brown and milky as chocolate
He smelt of creamy fruit salad
His name is Milky Mockolate.

His teeth were brown and jagged
Just like his body, all slimy
His hands were purple and tiny
His feet were huge, green and grimy.

He got out of his enormous rocket
He said, 'I'm as light as a balloon
Come and travel with me in space
We can visit the moon.'

Gabrielle Rawson (8)
John F Kennedy Primary School, Washington

Runners

Runners burst out of their blocks.
Faster, faster and faster they get
Faster than a speedin' jet.

Runners get into their stride.
Faster, faster and faster they are
Faster than a Jaguar.

Runners take over their opposition.
Faster, faster and faster they go
Like an arrow from a bow.

Runners go over the finish line.
Slower, slower and slower they get
Like a landing jet.

The race is over!

Reece McMann (10)
John F Kennedy Primary School, Washington

The Funny Alien

The funny alien is coming,
He is green as goo,
And he's coming for you!
He is coming . . .

The funny alien is coming,
His teeth are unclean like a rusty machine,
His jokes are very mean,
He is coming . . .

The funny alien is coming,
His laughter is so funny,
Even the space bears laughed and dropped their honey,
He is coming . . .

When he landed on Earth,
He spoke his language that sounded like cuckoo!
But then the people looked at him,
And put him in a zoo!

Rhys Buckham (9)
John F Kennedy Primary School, Washington

Rainforest

R arer animals are dying,
A ll of their food is destroyed,
I n the forests all the food is gone,
N ow animals are dead.
F orests are very old,
O n the animals there was blood,
R are animals are all cold.
E verything is in trouble,
S ea creatures are all dead too,
T rees are cut down too.

Daryl McMahon (7)
John F Kennedy Primary School, Washington

Space Monster

A monster landed here on Earth,
His face was as green as grass,
The monster found what his travel had been worth,
He's the biggest thing I've ever seen.

A monster landed here on Earth,
His legs were dark green,
He looked at me, then walked away,
I think he realised he had been seen.

A monster landed here on Earth,
He decided to do a bit of singing,
The singing gave me a headache,
Then my ears stopped ringing.

Liam Noble (9)
John F Kennedy Primary School, Washington

Who Has Seen The Wind?

Who has seen the wind?
Neither you nor I
But when leaves on the tree swirl away
You know the wind is flying by

Who has seen the wind?
Neither I nor you
The wind howling through open windows
It makes my head go blue

Who has seen the wind?
Neither you nor I
When it howls through my door
I can smell apple pie.

Christopher Johnson (9)
John F Kennedy Primary School, Washington

Once Upon A Time

Once upon a time
There was a rhyme
About a businessman
And guess what he ran?
A butcher's shop
That sold lamb chop.

He had a pink face
And it was a disgrace.
He had four chins,
He was more dirty than the bins.
He had a handle bar moustache,
All he cared about was cash.

He had a big round belly
That shook like a bowl of jelly.
He was grotty,
He had a wife called Lottie.
His height was four foot nine,
You'd think he lived in slime.

He was short and plump
And was very dumb.
He cried for his mummy
When he had an empty tummy.
Big fat fingers,
At the store his ghost lingers.

He spoke like Pavarotti singing,
All the time the doorbell was dinging.
He was harmless
But charmless.
He was never fired
Because he was desired.

Alexander Maddison (10)
John F Kennedy Primary School, Washington

An Alien

The alien is as pink as a pig,
Then he went, then he came,
Then he put on a rusty wig,
His back is red and purple.

The alien has white hair like a sheep,
He went outside and he saw brown as a cow,
When he went back in his house it was yellow,
Then he went in his bumpy bed.

The alien has red eyes as blood,
He went to his bed again and it was brown,
He'd do something if he could,
He did something, so he put on a crown.

The alien has ears as purple as a balloon,
He looked at something white,
Then he looked away,
Then he looked at the window and it was light.

Jade Walmsley (9)
John F Kennedy Primary School, Washington

I'm Not Telling

I know something you don't know
And I'm not telling.
I know something you don't know
And I'm not telling.

It crawls around at night,
Eats children in one bite.
I know something you don't know
And I'm not telling.

It's creeping up on you,
What are you going to do?
I know something you don't know
And it's too late in telling.

Natalie Taylor (10)
John F Kennedy Primary School, Washington

The Alien's Spacecraft

One day on Tuesday the fifth
An alien's spacecraft landed,
It was made of metal and had a lift,
Somebody was shouting inside it like a cackling witch!

The door swung open and a figure hopped out,
I saw green hair and a great big mouth,
The thing walked a little closer and I saw it had a snout,
Then the thing came into view and started to scream and shout!

He had a long neck like a giraffe,
Big purple warts and he ate glass,
His eyes were as cold as his laugh
And his name was Bibobath!

Then he hopped back into his strange spacecraft,
Closed the door and chucked something out,
I picked it up and pulled it out,
He had given me a frilly pink cap!

Sophie Jordan (9)
John F Kennedy Primary School, Washington

The Alien

The alien was as tall as a tree,
Not two eyes but three.

He walks alone at midnight,
Hoping to give children a fright.

He is pink and looks like jelly,
But he has a big fat belly.

His hair is as blue as the sea,
His hair was wet and it dripped on me.

His teeth were pink just like his body
And his name was Noddy!

Alex Hair (9)
John F Kennedy Primary School, Washington

The Alien In My Attic

I moved into a new home,
It was as big as a school,
On that night I wrote a poem,
Then I heard a noise from the attic.

I went out of my blank room,
I went up to the creaky stairs
That led up to the black attic tomb,
I put my hand on the cold handle and opened the door.

I heard some loud crunching
Behind the old brown cupboard,
It was very dusty and that thing was still munching,
That's when I met . . . the alien!

This is what he looked like,
He kind of looked like Mike,
His hair was dark brown,
He was blue with yellow spots.

The alien started to gurgle and slurp,
It was really loud,
Now he's going to burp!
It was really disgusting!

I started to scream,
I shouted,
'Alien,'
And the alien was never seen again.

Amy Richardson (8)
John F Kennedy Primary School, Washington

Space Monster

Once in outer space
A strange spacecraft hovered,
It had an ugly face
Which looked like it
Couldn't be bothered.

Inside was an alien
As crafty as can be,
The spacecraft's radar is failing
And now we cannot see.

The spacecraft was stopping,
Just like a slowing car.
The aliens' eyes were popping
Which looked quite bizarre.

The spacecraft was fine,
It was just the alien screaming,
It was actually the sun's bright shine
Which was extremely steaming.

The alien saw a meteor
Which scared him a lot,
So he used his brain
And gave it a shot.

The alien spacecraft blew up
Because he aimed in the wrong direction,
He won the biggest explosion cup,
I think the alien has lost its protection.

Brent Bradbury (8)
John F Kennedy Primary School, Washington

The Alien Outside The Door!

I woke up in my bed last night
Because I heard a sudden sound,
Those kinds of sounds
When your heart gives a thundering pound.

I walked over to my door
And got a dreadful fright,
Because of course it was
A most revolting sight.

It was an alien that I saw
Standing at my door,
It was the most scariest thing
I ever saw.

Then suddenly it opened
Its huge, slimy mouth like a wild, hungry lion,
Gobbled me all up
And I went flying down south
And that was that!

Emma Brewer (9)
John F Kennedy Primary School, Washington

Scared!

Friends are meant to stick by you,
Family are meant to hug,
So why am I sitting here alone,
Deserted like a bug?

No one here to reassure me,
Nobody here to care,
All alone with an itchy head,
It's just not fair.

'Next,' came the voice from the medical room,
From my class I was first,
My heart plummeted as I entered the room,
The room of the nit nurse!

Victoria Whitehead (10)
John F Kennedy Primary School, Washington

Our Fish's Life

Our fish's life is not very good,
There's just not much to it.

He swims around his little plant,
Pushes the glass for the fifty-sixth millionth time,
That he can't get through it.

Our fish's life is not very good,
There's just not much to it.

It's about the most boring life in the *world!*
He sleeps and he eats, he eats, eats, eats!
And I think he drinks, it drives me bonkers.

Our fish's life is not very good,
There's just not much to it.

You'd think it would drive him bonkers,
Swimming round and round his little plant.
It's certainly driving me bonkers
Watching him do it.

But he may be thinking, *that girl's life,*
There's not much to it, not much to it.

Watching a fish go round a plant,
It's driving me bonkers if only she knew it,
Watching she, watching me do it.

Parisa Asl (10)
John F Kennedy Primary School, Washington

Wonderful World

W e are spoiling our wildlife,
O ur world is going to die,
R oots and plants are rotting away,
L et the mammals live,
D ying is not what we want for the wonderful world.

Sophie Henderson (7)
John F Kennedy Primary School, Washington

I Don't Know What To Do?

I am sitting writing a poem,
But I want to be at home.
So what shall I do?
I haven't a clue.

I could write about a bun,
Or the sun.
So what shall I do?
I haven't a clue.

I could ask my mum,
But I'd rather twiddle my thumb.
So what shall I do?
I haven't a clue.

I could sit and think,
But I'd rather have a drink.
So what shall I do?
I haven't a clue.

I know, I'll write about my cousin Billy,
But that sounds silly.
So what should I do?
I haven't a clue!

Hannah Thompson (11)
John F Kennedy Primary School, Washington

Sports Car

S is for spoiler.
P is for Porsche.
O is for open top.
R is for rally.
T is for terrific car.
S is for suspension.

C is for car.
A is for amazing.
R is for racing.

Jordan Dixon (10)
John F Kennedy Primary School, Washington

I Want, I Want . . .

I want a green dinosaur, roaming around the street,
No! It will be too big!

I want a fire-breathing dragon, out in the garden,
No! It will dig!

I want a magical unicorn, walking peacefully in white,
No! It has a big horn!

I want a scaly fish, swimming the unknown,
No! I will have to feed it every morn!

I want a messy dog, getting muddy in the grass,
No! It will chase the postman!

I want a furry rabbit, sitting in his hutch,
No! It might get run over by a van!

I want a squeaky parrot, singing in his cage,
No! It will keep me awake!

No, perhaps I'll have *no one!*

Lauren Southern (10)
John F Kennedy Primary School, Washington

Environment

E very day I think how fantastic it is to be a tree,
N o noise and all my friends around me.
V iew is absolutely brilliant, all the trees talking to me,
I just love the air blowing past me.
R ound me things are really starting to get different,
O n the road there are cars rushing past me,
N ow all my friends have gone and there is not much wildlife,
M any houses and buildings are being built around me,
E very one of my friends has gone, I'm feeling all alone,
N ow there is no wildlife left,
T hings are getting dreadful for me, it's not so fantastic being a tree.

Charlotte McIntosh (8)
John F Kennedy Primary School, Washington

Food Fight At The Restaurant

At dinner time
I started a food fight.
I threw water at my brother,
I threw mushy peas at my sister.

I threw carrots at my mam,
I threw gravy at my dad.
I threw turnips at my auntie,
I threw cabbage at my uncle.

I threw cauliflower at my grandma,
I threw potatoes at my grandad.
I threw mint sauce at the waiter,
I threw chicken at the waitress.

And when it was time for dessert,
Well let's just say it was on me!

Victoria Graham (11)
John F Kennedy Primary School, Washington

Why?

'Just a moment.'
'Why?'
'Because I want to get my breakfast.'
'Why?'
'Because I am hungry.'
'Why?'
'Because I haven't had my breakfast.'
'Why?'
'Because I have just got up!'
'Why?'
'Because I was asleep.'
'Why?'
'Just stop saying *why*!'
'Okay what?'

Jordan Foley (10)
John F Kennedy Primary School, Washington

I'm Popping Over There

'I'm popping over there.'
'Popping where?'
'Over the road,
Popping back,
Then I'm popping to work.'
'Why are popping here and there?'
'I'm popping there so I can go to the fair.'
'Pop there tomorrow.'
'No, got to get popping.'
'Why?'
'Because I've got to work so I can get money.'
'Why?'
'Because I'm going on holiday.'
'Why holiday?'
'So I can get away from you.'
'Why away from me?'
'Because you're a pain in the neck.'
'Fine I'll pop there tomorrow.'

Robert Lloyd (10)
John F Kennedy Primary School, Washington

Environment

E very day I watch and talk with my friends,
N ever stop talking with my friends in the garden,
V iew is great and the trees are green.
I have a lovely breeze, fresh air all around me.
R ound me things are starting to grow,
O n the road it's starting to change,
N ow we do not have many trees anymore,
M any houses have been built near me,
E very tree has been suffocating,
N ow there is only a couple of us,
T hings are going to be lonely on my own.

Rhys Duffner (8)
John F Kennedy Primary School, Washington

The Gogglebot

The gobblebot is big and blue,
The gobblebot is furry too.

The gobblebot has a big round belly,
The gobblebot doesn't like jelly.

The gobblebot hates the light,
The gobblebot comes out at night.

The gogglebot has big black toes,
The gogglebot has no nose.

The gogglebot has three tails,
The gogglebot is scared of nails.

The gogglebot eats mice,
The gogglebot is not very nice.

The gogglebot ate a girl called Lor,
It has a big roar!

Victoria Doran (9)
John F Kennedy Primary School, Washington

Environment

E very day I think how brilliant it is to be a tree,
N o noise, just nice and peaceful.
V iew is beautiful, it is so good every tree in the world would
   like to be me.
 I have a lovely fresh breeze and great clean air,
R ound me I am getting quite upset, things are starting to change,
O n the roads it used to be grass instead.
N ow there isn't very much wildlife,
M any houses are being built and it is getting very noisy,
E very one of my friends has gone, I am so lonely,
N ow there is no one to talk to,
T hings are getting so terrible, I wish I was in another garden,
   I am not so lucky to be a tree.

Craig Foster (7)
John F Kennedy Primary School, Washington

Strangers In The Park

When I walked down to the park
I noticed an old Noah's ark.
Then I walked a little further
And saw a very creepy lurker.
I found out it was a wicked witch
And she threw me down a deep, dark ditch.
At last appeared a leprechaun,
'Hello,' he said, 'you're looking forlorn.'
This little fella was really strong,
'Come on,' he said, 'I'll help you along!'
He helped me out,
He was small but I had no doubt.
Then he walked me home
And I found that I was not alone
For my mam was there.
'Where have you been?' was all that she said.
'Now come inside, get ready for bed!'

Jordan Batey (10)
John F Kennedy Primary School, Washington

Environment

E very day it is so quiet and it is comfortable.
N o noise at all and it is so peaceful.
V iew is perfect and clear and fresh.
I have got an excellent breeze and I have got the
   wind blowing on me.
R ound me everything is changing and trees are being cut down.
O n the road it is tarmac and some of my friends have gone.
N ow there is not much wildlife and birds.
M any houses are getting built and I am so lonely,
   nobody is going past me.
E verybody is enjoying themselves.
N ow Sam has gone away and now I have got nobody.
T hings are terrible around me because I have no friends, after all.

Jack Short (7)
John F Kennedy Primary School, Washington

Dream Island

Far away in a
Distant land,
An island that
Is full of sand.

Trees of green,
Streams of blue,
There is a little
Person, it could be you.

Over the sea a
Ship sails ahoy,
Looking for
Treasure is a little boy.

The sun is golden,
Really warm,
On this island
There is no harm.

Palm trees shadow
Over the sand,
This is a
Gorgeous land.

Christina Savage (10)
John F Kennedy Primary School, Washington

Springtime

Springtime is a blooming blossom,
A newborn butterfly.
Springtime is a rose petal,
A lovely hot sun.

Springtime is a child's laughter,
A baby's first words.
Springtime is a child's play,
A baby's scream.

Cristal Robinson (9)
John F Kennedy Primary School, Washington

Environment

E very day is a very lovely day for me,
N o things are happening to make me sad.
V iew around me is really great, I have got lots
  of other trees to talk to.
I love being a tree because there is nature around me.
R ound me things are getting really, really different these days,
O n the grass lots of plants have disappeared around me,
N ow noise is coming from every direction, it is getting too rowdy,
M aybe it is not so great being a tree.
E very day things are changing so much for me,
N ow things are getting really lonely, all my best friends are gone.
T his is getting really horrible for me, things are getting noisier by
  the minute and my bestest friend Sam is moving away,
  I am very, very upset.

Emma Povey (7)
John F Kennedy Primary School, Washington

Environment

E very day my life as a tree is peaceful and quiet, I am so lucky,
N ot one minute goes by when I am lonely or unhappy.
  The air is fresh and warm.
V iew is gorgeous, trees, nature and my friends the plants,
I have many different places to look around.
R ound here lots of things have changed. Less birds, less trees
  and less animals.
O ver there is some tarmac roads, there is a fence trapping me,
N ow all my friends have disappeared.
M any houses and buildings are being built,
E very day something changes or moves.
N ow my friend Sam is moving away with his friends.
T errible things are happening, I can't breathe.
  Now I am not very lucky to be a tree.

Faye Chenery (7)
John F Kennedy Primary School, Washington

Something I Love About You

You. I love about you . . .
Your lovely sparkling blue eyes,
Your comforting smile on a night,
Your long blond hair on your head,
    Please I love you.

Your health is always loved,
I keep you in warmth and always will.
Now awaken, now,
    I'm waiting to
    Love you.

Don't go, please stay, I love you so.
I miss about you lots of things,
    I miss
    Everything.

Samantha Derrick (9)
John F Kennedy Primary School, Washington

My Why Poem

Why do we wear clothes?
Why do we go to school?
Why do birds fly?
Why do fish swim?
Why do flowers have scent?
Why do we have colours?
Why do we have subjects?
Why do we have letters?
Why do we have TV?
Why do we have a brain?
Why do we have countries?
Why do we live in houses?
Why do I always say why?

Kirstie Sloan (9)
John F Kennedy Primary School, Washington

The Circus

We went to the circus on Saturday,
We watched the acrobats swing and sway.

The juggling clowns gave us a laugh
And then I thought I saw a giraffe.

The lion let out an enormous roar
And I saw his monstrous jaw,
He had an enormous paw
That could cover the floor.

They had an elephant
Which killed a pheasant,
It had a massive paw
That crushed the floor.

Then people gave applause,
It was for a good cause.

Andy Johnson (10)
John F Kennedy Primary School, Washington

My Pet

My pet sleeps all day until the end of May,
She barks when someone comes through the door,
Then she goes to bed and snores.

My pet is lazy and dazy and she always says,
'My bed's too comfy so let me go to sleep,'
And then we take a little peep.

My pet is a hard dog and when she pulls on her lead
We always end up falling on a log.

My dog says that it's time to say goodbye
So we'll see you another day
But I ask why?

Natasha Cullerton (10)
John F Kennedy Primary School, Washington

My Auntie Sue Is My Favourite

My auntie Sue is my favourite for she can
Do the splits,
Catch me
And even paint the walls and read.

My auntie Sue is my favourite for she can
Run around,
Jump
And even fly.

My auntie Sue is my favourite for she can
Ride a motorbike,
Catch me
And even jump, skip and hop at the same time.

But the best thing is
That's she's
My auntie Sue!

Chloe Hesketh (10)
John F Kennedy Primary School, Washington

The Eagle

In a slimy cave
the eagle slept in its grave,
suddenly it spread out its wings
and went to look for mice and things.

It flew through the sky
watching the world go by,
set its eyes on a mouse
which disappeared into a house.

Then after a hard day
it went home with its prey
trapped in its beak,
that would last him to the end of the week.

James Reay (11)
John F Kennedy Primary School, Washington

Your Brandon, My Brandon

My Brandon's cuter than your Brandon.
Yes, your Brandon is I daresay.
If he gets any uglier he'll have to stay in a different room,
He won't be able to play.

Yes, but my Brandon's cleverer than your Brandon.
My Brandon's cleverer OK,
He knows his two times tables
And he is only three.

Ah, but my Brandon's got more hair than yours.
My Brandon's got more alright,
He's growing it for the winter,
It won't be a pretty sight.

Yes, but my Brandon's funnier than your Brandon,
If he starts laughing he never stops,
When he can't get to sleep at night
He has to drink his pop.

But my Brandon's friends with your Brandon.
Mine is friends with yours too.
They don't mind their mam and dad as long as they play
with each other.
I suppose that is true.

Emily Allan (11)
John F Kennedy Primary School, Washington

Once Upon A Rhyme

Once on the first spring morning
When everything came alive,
Lambs newborn,
Butterflies crack from their cocoons,
The time when new animals are born,
This is a lovely spring morn.

Laura Doran (9)
John F Kennedy Primary School, Washington

All Of My Friends

One of my friends is really tall,
One of my friends is really small,
One of my friends is a pain in the neck,
One of my friends always says heck.

One of my friends is very fair,
One of my friends has too much hair,
One of my friends wears a hat,
One of my friends is always up for a chat.

One of my friends is very funny,
One of my friends acts like a bunny,
One of my friends has smelly socks,
One of my friends always eats chocs.

One of my friends thinks she's got magic powers,
One of my friends even eats flowers,
One of my friends is nice and kind,
One of my friends does not mind.

One of my friends is only seven,
One of my friends wants to go to Heaven.
That's all my friends, I have no more
Until I walk through another door.

Leanne Markham (11)
John F Kennedy Primary School, Washington

The Cinema

I was at the cinema when nobody was about
But then I heard a great big shout.
Then I went out to explore,
Suddenly I heard somebody slam the door.
Soon I found I was locked in,
Then I saw a sharp pin.
I looked behind, somebody was there,
I tried really hard not to stare.

Sarah Warde (9)
John F Kennedy Primary School, Washington

Friendship Forever

I saw a man walking down the road,
Walking, walking with his load,
He saw me going the other way,
This is what he began to say.

He said to me, 'I need some help,'
I looked at the load and gave a yelp.
I said to him, 'That load's too heavy for me to carry,
I know who will help me, I'll call for Larry.'

Larry came and said to me, 'What is it dear,
What do you need?'
'This load's too heavy for me to carry,
Please help me my darling Larry.'

So we helped the man carry his load,
He began to walk down the road.
He disappeared out of sight,
As he walked past the moonlight.

Sophie Sanderson (10)
John F Kennedy Primary School, Washington

The Sun Was Shining

The sun was shining,
The sky was bright,
The waves were crashing
With all their might.
Mums were bathing
And paddling their toes,
Everyone having fun as it shows.

The sand was blowing,
The wind was strong,
All of a sudden the people were gone,
The beach was deserted.
The weather sent them away,
Maybe they'll come back another day.

Jade Illingworth (11)
John F Kennedy Primary School, Washington

Magic Box

(Based on 'Magic Box' by Kit Wright)

I will put in the box . . .
A baby dragon on the top of a tree,
A flying car machine to take me to the top of the sky,
A time machine to let me go back to my past.

I will put in the box . . .
A magic star that twinkles like silver in the darkest night,
A chalice of cold, crystal clear, sparkling water,
The multicolours of a treasured rainbow.

I will put in my box . . .
A money tree providing golden coins,
A house is made of gold,
A crazy world is made of gold.

I will put in my box . . .
A funny person with a magic pencil,
A crazy kid that's always making jokes,
The magic box full of secrets!

Ka Ho Law (11)
John F Kennedy Primary School, Washington

The Milky Bay

Whales drink pizza along the fish sticks
While dogs argue in Parliament.
The snail and slugs do magic tricks
And rabbits give up carrots for Lent.

If you go along the Milky Bay
You will surely want to stay.
If you stop and take a peek
It will be one you'll want to keep.

Ross Spalding (11)
John F Kennedy Primary School, Washington

My Dad

Eat, eat, eat,
Snore, snore, snore,
That's my dad - what a bore!

Sitting in his chair
Drinking his beer.
His football team scores - he gives a big cheer!

Watching the TV,
Smoking a ciggie,
You should see his belly - it's a biggie!

Lazes about,
Goes burp, burp, burp.
When he drinks you hear slurp, slurp, slurp!

Never washes,
Never cleans,
Doesn't have a clue what *tidy* means.

He doesn't do laundry,
He doesn't do cooking,
He lets our dog clean his plate when he thinks no one's looking!

Cold beans on burnt toast,
A takeaway on our lap,
Just before he has another nap!

Now I know he's not perfect,
Well, not even fine,
But he is my dad -

He's not yours - he's mine!

Jennifer Donnison (11)
John F Kennedy Primary School, Washington

Gorgeous Grub

Lemons are sour,
Strawberries are sweet,
Cheese can be pongy and smell like my feet.

Melons are juicy and apples are too,
But not the baked beans,
I think they are poo.

Ice cream and sweeties
Fresh from the shop,
Chocolate and chips
And glasses of pop.

Bananas and oranges,
Kiwi fruit too,
But not smelly jelly which looks like green goo.

These are the things I put on my plate,
Everything else I absolutely *hate!*

Daisy Wells (10)
John F Kennedy Primary School, Washington

Why?

'I'm just going to the supermarket.'
'Why?'
'Because I'm hungry.'
'Why?'
'Because we haven't had any shopping
since last week.'
'Why?'
'Because my boss hasn't given me any
money since last week.'
'Why?'
'Because that's the system.'
'Why?'
'High time you stopped saying why time.'
'What?'

Jonathan Edwards (10)
John F Kennedy Primary School, Washington

Funny People!

One person likes the sun,
Another person looks like a bun,
While someone else can always cheat
And their friend looks like a big treat.

Some people do lots of maths
While others like giraffes.
Another one has a lot of money
While someone else has a big fat tummy.

One person has a horrible pen,
Another person has a grandad called Len.
While someone else has a lovely dress,
Someone else made a huge mess.

Danielle Stone (11)
John F Kennedy Primary School, Washington

Footballers

Beckham is quite tall,
Owen's very small,
Ronaldo is a funny bunny,
Henry always thinks of his tummy

Lumberg has blond hair
Although he doesn't care.
Shearer is a brainy box,
Rooney has smelly socks.

Bellamy has brown eyes,
Seaman has lots of ties.
Giggs doesn't like camels
But doesn't mind other mammals.

Heskey has Reebok shoes,
Phillips leaves lots of clues.

Dean Finch (10)
John F Kennedy Primary School, Washington

My Friends

Sammy is a funny bunny,
Flex is small but a little tall,
Page is a small bean,
Popit is small but a little bit tall.

Fish is very tall but he likes the tank,
Camel likes camels but he smells a bit.

Pross is a cross,
Nickle has a short neck,
Spickle likes football but he likes Sunderland.

Sanny is shy but a little sly,
Hammy likes chicken but he likes ham better,
Frickle has won the trophy.

Hire like to fire but he also likes to desire,
Mike the magic fire has your great desire,
Phil had a little pill.

Zip and zip it more,
Simmy likes limy,
Lit likes the toilet,
Maddy likes his daddy
But he also likes his mammy.

Jord has a Ford,
Homer likes to hoover,
Billy is a bit silly,
John has a horn,
Clown has a crown.

Niall Mullen (10)
John F Kennedy Primary School, Washington

Snowflake

The glistening stars
Are like stabs of light in the night sky,
With painful glows
And white blood trickling slowly, slowly down . . .

The blood continues pouring into the world below,
Hanging in the night sky like a silver blur,
Creating a painful sting,
As the blood spilling faster, faster down . . .

The world like a guard,
Watching the blood fall silently,
Preventing it from falling further,
The blood is slower,
                    slower,
                        slower,
                            stop.

Kirsty Dodd (11)
John F Kennedy Primary School, Washington

Adventure Through A Rainforest

Open your eyes
What a wonderful surprise
The giant trees
Blowing in the light breeze
A colourful soft bird lands on my arm
It's feeling very calm

The warm rain starts to fall
The bird's mother makes a call
The wild plants all around
But there is still much more to be found

The hot sun starts to set
Time to say bye to the bird I met
Now it's time to set up camp
And light a fire because we are damp.

Laura Conley (9)
Ludworth Primary School, Ludworth

The Blazing Vulcan

(Written in the style of 'Jabberwocky' by Lewis Carroll)

'Twas dark and the mysterious volcano
Did smoke and burn in the night;
All frightened were the Romans
And the scared children cried.

Beware Vulcan, my son!
The tools that slam, the wings that flap!
Beware the Roman fire god and shun
His blacksmith's burning furnace.

One, two! One, two! and through and through
The burning volcano went rumble, boom!
Vulcan left it erupting and with his wings
He went flying back.

'Twas dark and the mysterious volcano
Did smoke and burn in the night.
All frightened were the Romans
And the scared children cried.

Scott Carter (10)
Ludworth Primary School, Ludworth

The Amazing Rainforest

In the rainforest the birds fly high
Up above the light blue sky.
Frogs are hopping
Bats are swinging
Down on the rainforest ground
Where bees buzz all around
Hope they don't fall straight to the ground.

Plants are growing by the trees
Yellow and black all around
Buzzing bees can be found
Animals are hopping across the ground
And birds are flying all around
The blue sky watches the clouds float by.

Daniel Rowlinson (8)
Ludworth Primary School, Ludworth

Pele The Fire God

(Written in the style of 'Jabberwocky' by Lewis Carroll)

'Twas dark and the scorching volcano
Did blaze and scorch in the midnight hour.
All screaming were the Hawaiians
And the children screamed with their mothers.

Beware the Pele my son! The hair that scorches
The voice that screamed beware the Hawaiians
And shun her dancing fire daughters!

One, two! One, two! And through and through
The powerful volcano went bang, clang!
Left it to blaze
And with her scream she went dancing back.

'Twas dark and the scorching volcano
Did blaze and scorch in the midnight hour.
All screaming were the Hawaiians
And the children screamed with their mothers.

Rachel Stabler (10)
Ludworth Primary School, Ludworth

Beautiful Rainforest

Down in the beautiful rainforest there are lots of trees
They are spiky, they will hurt your knees.

Warm rain falling
Sun shining high
Making the rain sparkle
Falling, falling through the leaves.

The animals are running around
As the rain falls on the rainforest ground
All the carnivores are hunting for food
Hope the bees aren't in a mood.

The birds are flying high in the sky
And my word, what about the herd?

Liam Turnbull (7)
Ludworth Primary School, Ludworth

The God Pele

(Written in the style of 'Jabberwocky' by Lewis Carroll)

'Twas warm and the blazing volcano
Did flicker and twist in the night;
All frightened were the Hawaiians
And the spooked cats ran.

'Beware Pele, my son!
The eyes that glance and the hair that flies.
Beware the Hawaiian dancing god
And shun her deadly daughters!'

One, two! One, two! And through and through
The bursting volcano went crackle - pop.
Pele left it steaming and with her shriek
She went dancing back.

'Twas warm and the blazing volcano
Did flicker and twist in the night;
All frightened were the Hawaiians
And the spooked cats ran.

Ryan Turner (9)
Ludworth Primary School, Ludworth

The Wonderful World Of A Rainforest

Deep in the rainforest a wonderful waterfall,
An old, beautiful canopy thirty meters tall.
See the magnificent plants and trees,
The creatures, insects and bumblebees.

Fruit growing everywhere,
Hot rain in the air.
Trees standing all around,
Their roots flowing underground.
The incredible animals, giant cats,
Angel-headed dragons and tube-nosed bats.

The world of the rainforest is a magnificent sight,
The colours of the day still glisten in the night.

Kieran Reay (9)
Ludworth Primary School, Ludworth

Pele The God

(Written in the style of 'Jabberwocky' by Lewis Carroll)

'Twas dark and the large volcano
Did grip and blaze in the moonlight mist;
All apprehensive were the Hawaiians
And the brown dogs shivered.

'Beware Pele my son!
The eyes that glow and the legs that dance!
Beware the killing god
And shun her horrible heart.'

One, two! One, two! And through and through
The bulging volcano went bang, pow!
Pele left it bubbling and with a screech
She went blasting back.

'Twas dark and the large volcano
Did grip and blaze in the moonlight mist;
All apprehensive were the Hawaiians
And the brown dogs shivered.

Jonathan Sutherland (10)
Ludworth Primary School, Ludworth

Adventure In The Rainforest

The rainforest is a beautiful place
Trees stand tall reaching to the sky
I look at them and they look so high

Down on the forest ground
Fruit on the forest floor
All the colours of the rainbow I can see
Shining and glowing around me

Sunlight shining bright
Warm rain falling through the trees
Animals creeping through the leaves
The rainforest is such a wonderful place
It puts a smile on my face.

Andrew Jackson (8)
Ludworth Primary School, Ludworth

The Roman God

(Written in the style of 'Jabberwocky' by Lewis Carroll)

'Twas daylight and the tall volcano did burst
And flutter in the sun;
All frightened were the Roman gods
And all children were nervous.

'Beware of Vulcan, my son!
The hammer that flings, the chisel that dashes.
Beware of the Roman fire god
And shun away.'

One, two! One, two! And through and through
The dashing volcano went clutter and bang,
Left it crashing with stamping and screaming.

'Twas daylight and the tall volcano did burst
And flutter in the sun;
All frightened were the Roman gods
And all children were nervous.

Abbie-Leigh Maitland (9)
Ludworth Primary School, Ludworth

In The Wonderful Rainforest

In the wonderful rainforest
Birds are singing
Monkeys are swinging

In the wonderful rainforest
There are lots of colours
Like green, blue, yellow and red

The warm rain sparkling and falling again
Through the beautiful trees
The animals play
All day.

Anthony Dove (7)
Ludworth Primary School, Ludworth

Dancing Pele

(Written in the style of 'Jabberwocky' by Lewis Carroll)

It was daybreak and the scorching volcanoes
Did erupt and bang in the moonlight
All scorching daughter
And the volcano erupted with lava.

Beware Pele, my daughter
The eyes that glow, the lava, the mystery
Beware of the Hawaiians
And shun the blazing lava.

The blazing went crash and bang!
Pele left it sizzling
And with her storm
She went dancing back with laughter.

'Twas break and the scorching sun did break
And bang in the moonlight
All scorching were the children
Who screamed and the volcano erupted.

Jessica Rose Miller (9)
Ludworth Primary School, Ludworth

Life In A Rainforest

Life in a rainforest where the water will fall
Animals play and insects crawl
Where the bats fly at night and birds sing all day
The monkeys will swing and the trees will sway.

Down in a rainforest it is very, very hot
Further in the rainforest it rains quite a lot
Giant snails all around
Most are crawling on the ground.

Further in the rainforest the birds are asleep
When they wake up the moon will peep.

Marc Lee (8)
Ludworth Primary School, Ludworth

Hawaii

(Written in the style of 'Jabberwocky' by Lewis Carroll)

'Twas cool and the bursting volcano
Did leap and flicker in the moonlight;
All shaking were the Hawaiians
And the nervous children crying.

'Beware Pele, my son!
The dancing fingers that wriggle,
The mouth that sings!
Beware the Hawaiian blazing god
And shun her blazing daughters.

One, two! One, two! And through and through
The boiling volcano went slam - clam!
Pele left it leaping and with her scream
She went leaping back.

'Twas cool and the bursting volcano
Did leap and flicker in the moonlight;
All shaking were the Hawaiians
And the nervous children crying.

Stevie-Leigh Hall (9)
Ludworth Primary School, Ludworth

What Can I See?

Through the rainforest what can I see?
Trees and animals, lots of bees
Rainforest creatures crawling around
Down on the wet rainforest ground
Drip drop water running through the trees
Warm and sparkling, landing softly on the leaves
Beautiful plants, yellow and red, standing tall
Soft leaves fall down, down, down to the forest floor.

Bobbie Hall (8)
Ludworth Primary School, Ludworth

The Legendary Vulcan

(Written in the style of 'Jabberwocky' by Lewis Carroll)

'Twas midnight, and the ancient volcano
Did blaze and crackle in the darkness
All amazed were the Romans
And the baby cats weep.

'Beware, Vulcan my son!
The feather that flaps the chisel that cracks
Beware the Roman ancient god and
Shun his house size hammer.'

One, two and through and through
The mysterious Vulcan went crackle, twist
Vulcan left it sizzling and with his
Hammer her went swooping back.

'Twas midnight, and the ancient volcano
Did blaze and crackle in the darkness
All amazed were the Romans
And the baby cats weeped.

Andrew Whittle (9)
Ludworth Primary School, Ludworth

A Night To Remember

November the 5th is a night to remember.
Hurry over to see the pretty fireworks!
See the rockets zoom and shoot into the clear night sky.
Hurry to watch the Catherine wheels as they spin and hiss.
Watch the sparkles twinkling and changing colour.
Watch them shatter and fall like a shooting star.
Hear them bang and whoosh as they fly.
Hear them whizz into the sky.
That's how November the 5th is a night to remember.

Rebecca Morton (10)
Our Lady Of The Rosary RC Primary School, Peterlee

Summer Comes

Summer comes
    With flowers blooming
Summer comes
    With people playing
Summer comes
    With birds singing
Summer comes
    With ice pops melting
Summer comes
    With temperatures rising
Summer comes
    With the sun shining
Summer comes
    With hot sea splashing
Summer comes
    With barbecues sizzling
Summer comes with happy holidays.

Chelsea Walker (8)
Our Lady Of The Rosary RC Primary School, Peterlee

Bird

Fly high bird!
Soar in the wind, fly high, fly fast.
So fast you can touch the sky.
When you fly you can see that the world is a ball that we tread on.
The hills are like mounds
You can't even see bees or ants.
The people like you and I are just little dots
Horses and dogs are even smaller.

Charlotte Taylor (8)
Our Lady Of The Rosary RC Primary School, Peterlee

Cinderella

On fine day in the month of May
Cinderella sat weeping,
'I've just had a call to the prince's ball
But I must stay to do the housekeeping!'

Her sisters were mean and not at all keen
For they had seen her beauty,
'Wait here,' they said, 'or we'll lock you in the shed.'
For both of them wanted the booty.

'Help me! Help me! Somebody help me!'
Cried Cinders pounding the wall,
With a pop and a bang, the fairy sprang,
And said, 'You will go to the ball.'

Her wand she flicked and legs she kicked
There appeared a wondrous gown.
'If you play your cards right, this very night
You could end up with the crown.'

She cast a glimpse and caught sight of the prince
Looking exceedingly charming
The prince saw her, she caused a stir
Her loveliness quite alarming.

The fairy watched on and when the music was gone
They were just about to kiss . . .
'No Cinderella! That's my kind of fella!'
As she knocked them apart from their bliss.

'I can grant wishes and do your dishes
For the rest of your life.'
Then the prince smiled for a little while
And said, 'You'll be my wife.'

Catherine Hanlon (11)
Our Lady Of The Rosary RC Primary School, Peterlee

No More Television

Please Dad don't do this to me,
I cannot live without my TV.
I'll clean my shoes, I'll tidy my room,
I'll do anything and I'll do it real soon.

No Son, TV is no more,
I don't even know what it was built for,
Now go to your room and do not complain,
For too much TV will damage your brain.

I could not believe it, I was out of my mind,
What could I do? What could I find?
Read a book? Draw a picture?
Play a game? What a mixture.

Here's a book, it's so exciting,
It's all about trees and lightning,
Thunder here, flashes there,
Light and sound everywhere.

Wait a minute surely not,
I can't already have forgot,
Well I only have one thing to say,
Who needs TV anyway!

Johanna Wood (11)
Our Lady Of The Rosary RC Primary School, Peterlee

Food

F reezer foods piled up high
O ver the top and up to the sky
O ven chips, sausage rolls,
    chocolate puds, toads in the hole
D inner is served, the waitress brings it,
    lots of food and lots of things.

Jessica Hough (8)
Our Lady Of The Rosary RC Primary School, Peterlee

Winter Comes

Winter comes
    With snowflakes falling
Winter comes
    With children playing
Winter comes
    With icicles dripping
Winter comes
    With people slipping
Winter comes
    With boys and girls sledging
Winter comes
    With animals hibernating
Winter comes
    With snowmen standing
Winter comes
    Wit fingers stinging
Winter comes to freeze me to death
    Winter comes.

Rebecca Hinton (9)
Our Lady Of The Rosary RC Primary School, Peterlee

Summertime

S un is beaming in the quiet streets
U nusual people chat and meet
M ums and dads bathe on the sunbeds
M e and my friends play games in the shed
E arly mornings awoken by singing
R unning races take place and so far you are winning
T ime to put away all of the paddling pools
I t's time for the leaves to come off the trees
M ammies and daddies go back to work
E veryone is back to school.

Jessica Flanagan (11)
Our Lady Of The Rosary RC Primary School, Peterlee

Pets

Amy   'I want a pet, any kind will do
            But I'm not going to clean up the poo!

Amy   Can I have a dog?'
Mum   'Only if you take it for a jog.'

Amy   'What about a cat?'
Mum   'No, you will have an allergy to that.'

Amy   'How about a snake?'
Mum   'Yes, only if it's fake.'

Amy   'Well how about a horse?'
Mum   'You're joking of course.'

Amy   'Can I have a mouse?'
Mum   'It will get lost in this house.'

Amy   'What about a rat?'
Mum   'Now that's enough of that.'

Amy   'But monkeys are the best.'
Mum   'Oh will you stop being a pest.'

Mum   'I know, why don't you make a wish
           And when you come in you might have a fish.'

Ashley Bowdler (9)
Our Lady Of The Rosary RC Primary School, Peterlee

Winter

Winter comes with people sledging,
Winter comes with people slipping,
Winter comes with snowballs flying,
Winter comes with Christmas arriving,
Winter comes with babies crying.
That's what winter's all about!

Danny Wilson (9) & Ryan Cox (8)
Our Lady Of The Rosary RC Primary School, Peterlee

There's No One There

I walk into a damp, dark and dreary cellar.
I hear a blood-curdling screech,
a loud cry for help.
but there's no one there.
I walk a little further and hear the creaks on the wooden floor,
as if there were some other human in this haunted cellar.
I then feel a trickle of water run down my body.
I see creepy shadows which are moving slowly,
across the dank wall.
But what a surprise,
there's no one there.
Footsteps of the living dead approaching.
Looking at the trickling muddy water
running down from the cobwebbed roof,
it leads me to a face.
I look closer.
There is someone there, me!

Rachael Cooke (8)
Our Lady Of The Rosary RC Primary School, Peterlee

Life Under The Ocean

Down in the depths of the deep blue sea there lived . . .

Ten jumping jellyfish dancing daintily through the waves
Nine lovely lobsters hiding in the caves
Eight delightful dolphins giving people rides
Seven wonderful whales - swim for your lives
Six sad swordfish looking for a tasty meal
Five terrific turtles playing with a seal
Four pleasant piranhas looking for their prey
Three obedient octopus having a glorious day
Two super salmon diving up and down
One mysterious monkfish, who had quite a frown.

Michael Fortune (8)
Our Lady Of The Rosary RC Primary School, Peterlee

Summer

Summer comes with
    Flowers opening
Summer comes with
    Grass cutters trimming
Summer comes with
    The hot sun shining
Summer comes with
    Children paddling
Summer comes with
    Children swimming
Summer comes with
    Adults bathing
Summer comes with
    Birds chirping
Summer comes with
    People burning
        That is the spirit of summer.

Charlotte Flanagan (8)
Our Lady Of The Rosary RC Primary School, Peterlee

Under The Sea

Down in the depths of the deep blue sea lived . . .

10 dancing dolphins playing tag
9 sly sharks searching for their prey
8 bobbing jellyfish stopping bubbling about
7 small fish came out of the sea anemone
6 flat fish hiding underground
5 starfish sticking to the rocks
4 sea horses playing in the weed
3 sea turtles riding the East Australian current
2 big crabs hiding under the rocks
And 1 huge whale eating squid for the day.

Jamie Keen (8)
Our Lady Of The Rosary RC Primary School, Peterlee

My Bedroom

In my bedroom there are
10 ants
In my bedroom there are
9 beetles
In my bedroom there are
8 ladybirds
In my bedroom there are
7 mice
In my bedroom there are
6 frogs
In my bedroom there are
5 hedgehogs
In my bedroom there are
4 geese
In my bedroom there are
3 snakes
In my bedroom there are
2 lions
In my bedroom there is
1 elephant
So keep out.

Amanda Wilson (9)
Our Lady Of The Rosary RC Primary School, Peterlee

I Love Dolphins

I love dolphins
They are my friends
They swim in the ocean
Like whales.

I love dolphins
They are my friends
They are so cute
I love dolphins.

Stephanie Longstaff-Watson (9)
Our Lady Of The Rosary RC Primary School, Peterlee

Arthur

Arthur is my pet, he is also my friend,
The way he runs about his wheel drives me round the bend.
He is awake all night and sleeps all day,
All he wants to do is play.
He gobbles up his food and stuffs it in his pouch,
But sometimes my fingers get in the way and I shout *ouch!*
I love my little hamster, I pat his little head,
I love the way he snuggles up in his cotton wool bed.

Lucy Kemp (8)
Our Lady Of The Rosary RC Primary School, Peterlee

Autumn Leaves

A mazing autumn is here again
U nwanted autumn is here to stay
T he leaves are rustling in the breeze
U ntil the winter comes hiding in the breeze
M um's horrible casserole is back to haunt me again
N asty winter's here, but it will end just the same.

Cameron Finn (8)
Our Lady Of The Rosary RC Primary School, Peterlee

My Cat

My cat, my cat, my cat is black.
My cat, pounce and purr.
My cat, velvet fur.
My cat, emerald eyes.
My cat, silent lies.
My cat, soft paws.
My cat, sharp claws.
Pounce, purr, sleep and play,
Harry my cat you make my day.

Anna Minchell (9)
Our Lady Of The Rosary RC Primary School, Peterlee

Under The Sea

In the submarine
I could see a bright beam,
They all come towards me,
Every kind in my dream,
Small ones, big ones, large ones too,
It seemed so impossible from that small view.

As I got near the bottom
I could see a small pool,
Crabs, lobsters, starfish too,
It seemed like we were in the zoo,
Everyone staring and smiling at you.

Megan Wood (9)
Our Lady Of The Rosary RC Primary School, Peterlee

Bonfire Night

As I approached the burning fire,
I listen to the wonderful choir.
Here started the night,
Which gave me a horrible fright.

My baby cousin is in the water works,
Just like the fireworks.
Adults watch the choir,
As children enjoy the fire.

The burning sparklers in the night,
Is the bright guiding light.
Children shouting at the sight,
With people saying, 'What a night!'

Leanne Newton (11)
Our Lady Of The Rosary RC Primary School, Peterlee

Dolphins Are Like Diamonds

Dolphins are like diamonds, extremely rare,
Silky skins and not a strand of hair.
They shimmer in the sea as they dance through the waves,
They sparkle in the waters dazzling as they sway.
Dolphins are like diamonds, extremely wanted,
They are precious and desired and needed and craved.
Dolphins are like diamonds, extremely rare,
Silky skins and not a strand of hair.
They shimmer in the sea,
As they dance
Through the waves.

Samantha Brown (9)
Our Lady Of The Rosary RC Primary School, Peterlee

My Baby Sister

My baby sister is three,
She totally hates me.

My sister loves her peas,
She always tries to make me freeze.

My sister loves the snow,
She tries to say ho ho.

My sister is crazy,
She is very, very lazy.

When my sister goes to sleep,
You can never hear a peep.

Katie Nash (8)
Our Lady Of The Rosary RC Primary School, Peterlee

Seashell

Lift to your ear
Listen to country seas
Shapes are lovely like your dreams
Strange ocean fantasies
From all over the world
On beaches, on shore
Or even in the sea
Some are twirling and swirling
So original
So part of the beauty in the sea of seaweed.

Brogan Turner (8)
Our Lady Of The Rosary RC Primary School, Peterlee

Neale Family Fireworks

A Roman candle repeating, repeating all her gentle words -
my mum obviously.

A rocket shooting up with anger and is very impatient -
that's my dad.

A silver fountain giving and being very kind -
that would be by nanna.

A volcano that's just been lit and full of energy -
that's my grandad all right.

A golden rain very bright, happy and kind -
that's Kimberly.

I'm like a sparkler glowing, glowing brightly
until I'm dim and gone.

Melissa Neale (10)
Redesdale Primary School, Wallsend

Sparklers

Dancing sparks in the moonlight
Colours on sparkling sticks
Catch your eye
Fizzing flowers
Silvery shadows
Spitting, flicker and fiery
A blazing wand
In the night.

Gemma Charlton (11)
Redesdale Primary School, Wallsend

Sparklers

Sparks, sparks everywhere
Here to guide you through filthy air
Sparks dancing, sparks flying
Somewhere in the foggy air
Sparks here, sparks there, sparks, sparks everywhere
Gold, green, red and blue
Multicoloured to inspire you.

Ethan Rowan (11)
Redesdale Primary School, Wallsend

Clock

24 hour ticker,
Non-stop tocker,
Appalling alarm disturber,
Nuisance waker,
Time reminder,
Steady fellow,
Until the battery goes,
What am I?

Ketty Ho (11)
Redesdale Primary School, Wallsend

Shearer - Cinquains

Shearer!
Plays for The Toon.
Sir Bobby's best player,
Scores exquisite match winning goals,
Shearer!

Shearer!
Went to the club,
Where he was born, Wallsend,
Then he played for The Toon Army,
Shearer!

He plays
For the best team,
His fans support him well,
He used to play for Southampton,
Shearer!

Shearer
He is the best,
I wish I could meet him.
Scoring good goals for Newcastle,
Shearer.

Alex Robson (10)
Redesdale Primary School, Wallsend

The Schoolday

Get out of bed sleepyhead
It's schoolday today
Get some breakfast
Watch some TV
Then get my uniform
Put my coat on
Grab my bag
Knock on my mate's door
Walk to school with him
Then go in school and write some poetry.

Jonathan Campbell (11)
Redesdale Primary School, Wallsend

SATs - Cinquain

Oh no!
The SATs paper
My nerves are going wild
A cold shiver runs through my spine
I passed!

Dean Hamilton (11)
Redesdale Primary School, Wallsend

The Guy

I was minding my own business,
When some boys came round the corner.
They took me with a big bag of straw,
They took me to some bushes, with a big pile of wood.
I had a feeling this was not good.
Evening came, so did the boys.
They stuffed straw inside me.
They had matches, it was time for me to burn.
When I'm done being a costume
I want to know why this is happening.
    Will I learn?

Jake Young (10)
Redesdale Primary School, Wallsend

What Am I?

Coloured stripes
Forked tongue
Sharp teeth
I slither
I also live in grass
What am I?

Martin David Chambers (10)
Redesdale Primary School, Wallsend

Smith Family Fireworks

Amy's a rocket shooting past the moon with a big bang.
Carly's a hellraiser flying through the air exploding on the way.
Jay's a squealer, squealer in the sky, squealing louder and louder.
Karen's a Catherine wheel, spinning on the fence getting faster
                                                    and faster.
Mam's a sparkler, sparkling and crackling in my hand.
Dad's a banger, banging all night in the black sky.
I'm a missile command going up, getting faster and faster.

Dale Smith (11)
Redesdale Primary School, Wallsend

TV - Cinquain

TV
Television
Interesting programmes
Change a channel, watch a movie
TV.

Rose Stock (10)
Redesdale Primary School, Wallsend

The Bonfire

Everybody's gathering to see the bonfire,
Girls and boys laughing to see the big moment.
Couches, mattresses and straw piled up high,
The shape of a cone in the dusty sky.
As the bonfire is lit up people gaze with eyes as bright as the sun.
Sparks flying everywhere, burning brightly
Like a golden flare.

Lucy Quinn (11)
Redesdale Primary School, Wallsend

Bonfire

Bonfires are bright
You can get a fright
Flames can burn you
Chuck things in
And the flowers will grow
Bigger and bigger
People throw chairs
People chuck tables.

Phillip Elsdon (10)
Redesdale Primary School, Wallsend

Spiders' Webs Haiku

I like spiders' webs
Look at the dust on the webs
As they wrap flies tight.

Jamie Briggs (11)
Redesdale Primary School, Wallsend

Fire Engine

It's red and yellow, glows in the dark
Big bright blue lights
Which flash like mad
It's loud like a car horn
It puts out fire
Quick as a flash
Its big water pourer
Pours very fast
It can fill a pond
Nee-nor, nee-nor, it sounds all night.

Matthew Douglas (11)
Redesdale Primary School, Wallsend

The Bonfire

The flames start to rise
I feel the cries
Of the wood burning
It's getting hotter
And hotter
Is that me burning?
I'm boiling
I hear the cries
Of the fire dying
I can see colours
Of red, orange and yellow
Shooting to the sky
Now it's completely burned
And now I'm beginning
To realise the purpose
Of life again.

Adam Mishner (11)
Redesdale Primary School, Wallsend

The Newspaper Maker

Aluminium plates made with ink,
Using cian, magenta, yellow and black.
Rolls of paper which weigh a ton,
Using a skateboard to transport.

Conveyor belts like roller coasters,
Moving around the whole building.
Workers using squishy ear plugs,
So their ear drums won't burst.

Papers that have not been used,
Will be recycled in machines.
Each roll makes sixty thousand copies,
And only six seconds to print.

Jobie Lee (10)
Redesdale Primary School, Wallsend

Gittins' Family Fireworks

Carol's a shiny sparkler, sparkling day and night,
Terry's a crazy banger, popping non-stop.
Sean's a whizzing Catherine wheel, whizzing round the room.
Sam's a mental squealer, squealing all day long.
I'm an exploding volcano, spitting and erupting all day and night.
My nan's a silver fountain, bursting out her top.
You can always hear the pop!

Max Gittins (11)
Redesdale Primary School, Wallsend

Umbrella

When it's raining what do I use?
My umbrella
To keep the raindrops off my head
There's nothing I can use instead.

If I have got a cold and can't get wet, what do I use?
My umbrella.
Watching bright colours, apart from the rain
It's a brilliant way to walk so I'll use it again.

When it's raining what do I use?
My umbrella.

Sophie Wouldhave (11)
Redesdale Primary School, Wallsend

Sparklers

Fuzzy flowers
Dancing in the dark
Burning blossoms
What a lark!
Fizzing electricity
Like the sun shining bright
Hold them tightly while they're alight.

Marni Brennan (10)
Redesdale Primary School, Wallsend

Mullen Family Fireworks

Mum's like a sparkler, twinkling day after day.
Dad's like a loud rocket, shouting above the sky.
Samantha's like a tornado, squealing and banging.
Aaron's like a jigsaw, shooting up different colours.
Emma's like a Roman candle, mad then calm.

Emma Mullen (11)
Redesdale Primary School, Wallsend

The Desert

The bushes are bare with leaves on the ground
The small creatures are tummy-bound
The lion's roar shakes the land
While he prowls in the sand
Jackals eat leftover food
But when the lion's in a bad mood
He'll gobble them up too
But then you'll see a mystery creature, who?
It's the giraffe eating leaves from the highest tree
When they eat, it is free
A lot of animals eat each other
But when one is in danger, they join together.

Matthew Clark (10)
Redesdale Primary School, Wallsend

Clock Cinquain

Tick-tock
Time of the clock
Ticks all night, ticks all day
It must be right, it can't be wrong
Tick-tock.

Lauren Irving (10)
Redesdale Primary School, Wallsend

Hallowe'en Night

Costume wearing kids
Time has come for children's fun,
Masks and capes, sweets and treats,
Kids running, egging houses,
Until the end of the night!

Adam Nelson (11)
Redesdale Primary School, Wallsend

The Bonfire

It is quiet until a match is lit,
Then it springs to life.
It hisses and spits,
Reddy-orange flames sprout up
Into the pitch-black sky.
It cackles like a hyena,
Roars like a lion.
The rotting wood and chairs,
Ancient newspapers and cardboard boxes,
Burn most of the night.

Carl Reid (10)
Redesdale Primary School, Wallsend

Sparkler

They crackle and fizz like a fizzy lollipop,
The colour's like a bolt of lightning,
To some people they are very frightening,
They don't go high in the sky,
But very quickly the sparks will die.

Kristopher West (10)
Redesdale Primary School, Wallsend

The Beach Tanka

Playing in the sea,
You can sunbathe on the beach,
Flying your big kite,
You can take a picnic there,
With pop and nice sandwiches.

Rachel Tiplady (11)
Redesdale Primary School, Wallsend

Ho Family Fireworks

Dad is a sparkler, sparkling under the sky
He runs around like a man up high
Mum's a golden rain, whizzing down the lane
When my brother's hurt, she cures all the pain
Johnny's a rocket, bursting up high
Explodes and brings colour to the sky
Mark's a Roman candle, but he's hard to handle
He bursts with embers and lit his sandal
I am a banger, popping up to the sky
I whizzed up and the explosion is high.

Eric Ho (11)
Redesdale Primary School, Wallsend

Cliff - A Personification Poem

She lives next to the sea,
Children climb on her,
She is rocky but not slimy,
She wears a green dress,
Made out of seaweed,
People think it's a mess!

Valerie Wong (10)
Redesdale Primary School, Wallsend

The Bright Sun - Tanka

The sun shining down,
Upon the world it shines bright.
Throwing neat around,
Lovely warmth all round the world,
The sun dancing in the sky.

Cameron Spinks (10)
Redesdale Primary School, Wallsend

Evening

Brush your teeth, it's time for bed,
You must lie down and rest your head.
Outside the sky is pink,
Spit your toothpaste in the sink.
Climb into bed, I'll tuck you in,
When morning comes you can play with Lynne.

Morning comes,
Come on, let's go and play in the lane,
Sunrise has come again.

Anna Laws (10)
Redesdale Primary School, Wallsend

Gentle Waves

Such a soft flow
So you don't know
When the tide will turn
And the sun will burn
But the gentle waves will cool you
But don't let them fool you
The strong, gentle waves.

Laura Pollington (10)
Redesdale Primary School, Wallsend

Ramm Family Fireworks

Mam's a silver fountain,
Gentle and kind, white like the snow.
Dad's a banger,
Loud, jumping about and ready to go.
Yasmin's a Roman candle, always running,
Angry, flaring and shooting out.
Georgia's a volcano, smoking and scary,
Spitting and raging.
Grandma's a bright yellow fireball,
Shining like the sun.

Yasmin Ramm (10)
Redesdale Primary School, Wallsend

Autumn Haiku

The leaves fall from trees
And the magnificent trees
Look bare, dead and destroyed.

Luke Wilson (10)
Redesdale Primary School, Wallsend

King Of The Jungle Kennings

Loud roarer
Meat eater
Big cat
Jungle king

Orange mane
Light footed
Proud feast
Sharp teeth.

Katherine Hannett (10)
Redesdale Primary School, Wallsend

The Lion Kennings

Fuzzy mane
Loud roar
Fast runner
Zebra eater
Tawny tail
Strong body
Proud beast
King of the jungle.

Chelsea Watson (11)
Redesdale Primary School, Wallsend

Butterfly

I am flying high,
Up in the deep blue sky,
Pretty butterfly.

Geoffrey Robinson (10)
Redesdale Primary School, Wallsend

Briggs' Family Fireworks

Mum's like a rocket,
Always busy, never stopping.
Dad is like the sun,
Running and fixing things.
Ian is a Catherine wheel,
Callum's whizzing on his motorcycle.
Gran's a jigsaw,
Always loving and happy.
Tony reminds me of a Roman candle,
Sometimes angry, other times not.

Lewis Briggs (11)
Redesdale Primary School, Wallsend

Goodbye

I don't want to leave
So I hide my face in my sleeve
I am crying
I'm not lying
My friend wants to go
So he stamps on my toe
I bring out my face
And pretend to tie my lace
With my face red
I want to go to bed
I'm tired of standing
So I say farewell and go up to the landing.

Charlotte Valentine (10)
Redesdale Primary School, Wallsend

The Sneeze

At-at-atishoo!
I've got the flu
Snuggle in bed
I've got the sneezes
Said Doctor Ned
At-at-atishoo!
Got a pain too
Tummy tumbling
Me grumbling
R-r-rumble
I've got the tummy pain
Said Doctor Ned
No more
At-at-atishoo!

Bethany Watson (11)
Redesdale Primary School, Wallsend

Guy Fawkes

I sit in a grand high chair,
And I see people stare.
It's very cold, freezing even,
I see a boy called Steven.
Then I see bright red,
And see a burning bed.
I get very hot with orange and yellow,
I think I'm feeling very mellow.
My great hat falls off and my chair becomes tasty,
I feel very roasty.
I start to melt and it burns and burns,
But nobody turns or squirms.
And there and then I bend,
And then it is the end.

Jessica Sarin (10)
Redesdale Primary School, Wallsend

News Room

Monday the 17th of November,
We travelled out of school,
We each got computers, typing away,
I thought it would be boring for one whole day,
But I was wrong, computers are cool.

First we type in Ted,
Then we type in Fred,
Type the headline,
Lights off, listen,
Type in the caption,
We went on action,
We printed our papers,
Just in time.

Kieran Ho (10)
Redesdale Primary School, Wallsend

A Goldfish's Wish

I'm a pretty goldfish
And my deepest wish
Is to see my family
Living happily.

Until the dreaded day
Hand took me away
Carried me in hard air
Took me somewhere
That somewhere is here
Far from my home not near
In my lonely bowl
At the top a hole
I tried to get up
But the angry pup
Ferociously barked at me
He is so scary.

I'm a pretty goldfish
And my deepest wish
Is to see my family
We lived happily.

Josephine Leung (11)
Redesdale Primary School, Wallsend

Chips

How can you live without any chips?
Golden and shiny,
They're good for the hips,
Most aren't that tiny,
How can you live without any chips?

Norman Hunter (11)
Redesdale Primary School, Wallsend

Sparkler

Sparklers through the night,
Like a fizzy lollipop,
Crackling sparks come whooshing out,
Yellow and gold glitters in the black sky,
Sparks come out from the magic wand,
Lights up the dark sky in the black night.

Helen Fong (11)
Redesdale Primary School, Wallsend

Watson Family Fireworks

My dad is like a volcano, erupting red,
He storms around the house and snores in bed.
My mam is like a silver fountain, as calm as a cat,
She sorts things out for everyone and fixes things like that.
My brother's like a Roman candle who flames up at people,
He gives us all such a fright and certainly isn't little.
My grandma's like golden rain, she's really very quiet,
She doesn't get in people's way, unless they're making a riot.
I am like a sparkler with my eyes shining bright,
Until my brother comes up to me and gives me such a fright.

Sophie Watson (11)
Redesdale Primary School, Wallsend

Snow

Lying on tree tops,
Like a pearly-white blanket,
Spreading over lands,
Falling from the cloudy skies,
As cold ice balls or snowflakes.

Amy Sill (11)
Redesdale Primary School, Wallsend

The Deep Blue Cinquain

Roaring,
Creating waves,
Spreading across the globe,
Crashing and bashing against cliffs,
Clear, blue.

Michael Woodmass (10)
Redesdale Primary School, Wallsend

Sparklers

Sparks of every colour,
Crackling through the night,
Fizzing and whizzing through the air,
A bit like a fizzy lollipop,
That's twirling around on a stick,
Golden, red and yellow sparks,
Spitting off a stick,
Sparklers are so brilliant,
So make sure you watch them.

Emily Watson (11)
Redesdale Primary School, Wallsend

Clements' Family Fireworks

My dad is a big rocket who shouts over the hills.
My brother David is a Catherine wheel because he runs very fast.
My mum is a jigsaw who is calm and cool.
My brother Mark is a big bomber who explodes over the crowds.
And me, James, a squealer who shrieks over the buildings.

James Clements (11)
Redesdale Primary School, Wallsend

Turnbull Family Fireworks

Mum is a silver fountain,
    gentle as the rain.
Dad is a Roman candle,
    flaring up again.
Steven is a rocket,
    exploding unexpectedly.
Joe is a banger,
    booming effectively.
Grandad is a sparkler,
    never getting angry.
Nanna is a squealer,
    always worrying badly.

Lee Turnbull (11)
Redesdale Primary School, Wallsend

My Cat

Prowling hunter,
Always hungry,
White and ginger,
Can be angry.
    Pointy ears,
    Furry tail,
    Never in tears,
    He is male.
Meat eater,
Uses his claws,
Glow-in-the-dark eyes,
Door opener.

Thomas Lapworth (10)
Redesdale Primary School, Wallsend

Summer

Summer comes
    With birds singing,
Summer comes
    With my brother swinging.
Summer comes
    With butterflies flying,
Summer comes
    With worms dying.
Summer comes
    With people sunbathing,
Summer comes
    With my dad shaving.
Summer comes
    With me having fun, lovely summer.

Georgia Creasy (8)
Ryhope Junior School, Sunderland

Scary Night

Howling voices,
Squeaky noises.
Scary laugh,
Slippery path.
Spooky cobwebs.
I looked around,
I'm in someone's house.
I'm getting really scared.
Tarantulas all around me.
I'm getting terribly frightened.
I think I'm going to die.
But what's that over there?
It's a door,
I'm free.

Kristi Henson (8)
Ryhope Junior School, Sunderland

Bunnies

Bunnies, bunnies are so funny
Hopping all around the ground
They have fluffy black tails
That look like pom-poms
They like vegetables to eat
And have really big feet
They live in burrows in the ground
That's where they are found
Bunnies are mute
But they are so very cute.

Amy Hibbert (7)
Ryhope Junior School, Sunderland

Fireworks

Fireworks, fireworks they are bright
Sometimes they can give you a fright
You let them off with a big spark
In the dark.

Becky Clark (8)
Ryhope Junior School, Sunderland

Angry

I'm as angry as an erupting volcano,
Angry as a charging bull,
Angry as pepper,
I'm chilli angry,
I'm as angry as red,
Tomato-faced red,
As angry as a thunderstorm,
As angry as a fire siren,
I'll stamp, shout and scream.

Abby Cooper (10)
Ryhope Junior School, Sunderland

Grumpy

I'm as grumpy as an elephant
Stomping and grunting around
As grumpy as a grey sky
Grumpy like a tortoise
Watching my fellows play
While I sit in a dark corner of the room.

Allison Brettell (10)
Ryhope Junior School, Sunderland

Friends

My friends are funny and always happy
My friends are joyful but sometimes unhappy
Robin is a lovely girl
Leah is nice
Amy is a handful
But Danielle is fun
We are all good friends and cheerful too
We are helpful and kind when we are at school.

Stacey Sinclair (7)
Ryhope Junior School, Sunderland

Crazy Football

I like football because it is great
I like football, playing with my mate
I like Sunderland, because they are cool
I like football because it is great
I like football, playing with my mate
I like Real Madrid 'cause they are class
I like football, playing in school.

Lewis Anthony Storey (8)
Ryhope Junior School, Sunderland

Spooks

S cary houses in the town,
P oltergeist creeping up on clowns.
O range ogres creeping around,
O wls flying without a sound.
K iller bats hunting at night,
S cary ghosts fright.

James Hartley (9)
Ryhope Junior School, Sunderland

Playing In The Snow

Snow in the windows
Snow on the ground
Snow on the rooftops all around
As I go out and you all stay in
You, my brother, my sister and twin
I build a snowman for you and my brother
And a snow girl for my sister and mother
And last but not least, my little twin
We've got the best, the best is a tin
A tin full of chocolates, a tin full of taste
I think we're getting dirty, let's go and wash our face.

Hannah Barkel (8)
Ryhope Junior School, Sunderland

Happy

I'm as happy as a bubbling stream,
A blue bubbling stream.
As happy as the sun,
An updated toy.
I would be a winner,
Parading loudly,
Down the high street.

Ivan Godfrey (9)
Ryhope Junior School, Sunderland

Sad

I'm as sad as an elephant
Sad as blue!
Sad as a mashed potato
Sitting on a plate.

I'm as sad as rain
Sad as an overcoat
I'll weep, moan
And cry in pain.

Adam Kitching (9)
Ryhope Junior School, Sunderland

Cloud

The cloud is a polar bear in the ice blue Antarctic.
It is a scrumpled piece of paper in a blue bin.
A sheep's fleece in a dream.
It is candyfloss in a pink bag.

Nathan Riley (10)
Ryhope Junior School, Sunderland

Winter

Lamenting wind and falling snow,
Dark, dim nights, cold cheeks aglow.

Snowmen built and fires lit,
Wrapped up warm with scarves and mitts.

Noses red and small hands numb,
Mr Frost has obviously come.

Snowball fights and tall trees bare,
The howling storms may give you a scare.

Run, run to the safety of your house,
Like a small, scared, timid mouse.

Rebekah Ruddock (10)
Ryhope Junior School, Sunderland

The Mysterious Thing

The weird thing was really funny,
Do you know what was next to it, a large bunny.
Its hair was like rags,
It looked like it had been shopping with all the bags.
I wish I had a stick,
Then I'd give him a kick.
I would say he had 10 legs,
He ate loads of eggs.
But when I met it, he was as kind as my mam and dad,
But soon he got a bit mad.
He wore dungarees like Dennis the Menace,
And he played tennis.
It was as thin as a stick,
He wanted to give me a lick.
In the morning I was still there, so was he,
I found out he was an alien.

Bethany Allen (8)
Ryhope Junior School, Sunderland

Ssccrreeaamm

S pooky skeleton in the demon house,
S cary, dary devils are frightening a mouse.
C reepy creatures crawling on your body,
C alling wolves come out your potty.
R ivers with galloping headless horsemen,
R iddling rhymes sending you to Hell with the Manson men.
E at into your skin with vampires,
E vil is coming your way with chant fires.
A demon can course a spell with lies,
A lien Alice comes to the fires.
M edium mice chat nice,
M ad Manson is never nice so watch yourself tonight.

Demi Procter (8)
Ryhope Junior School, Sunderland

Summer

Summer comes
   with people diving.
Summer comes
   with water splashing.
Summer comes
   with the sun blazing.
Summer comes
   with diving boards springing.
Summer comes
   with birds whistling.
Summer comes
   with people sunbathing.
Summer comes
   with happy people,
Beautiful summer.

Glyn Lamb (8)
Ryhope Junior School, Sunderland

Ghost Train

In the carriage
I think I am going to be sick with porridge.
3, 2, 1, go,
Climbing up my seat.

A sudden stop,
My carriage pops,
Oh no I'm going backwards!

Howling wheels,
The skeleton keels.
Oh my God,
Then I noticed it was over.

Sarah Halsall (9)
Ryhope Junior School, Sunderland

Devil

Evil children
Vampires
Insane insects
Lone spirits walk along in the night
Ghost flying in the night
Footsteps creeping
Noises heard
Banging loudly.

Melainey Camsey
Ryhope Junior School, Sunderland

Winter Days

The snow is cold and is whistling,
And inside the house the pan is sizzling.
There was a big sneeze,
And the leaves fell off the trees.
The people play,
Now it is May.

Robyn Atkinson (9)
Ryhope Junior School, Sunderland

Winter Poems

Whistling wind
Round my head,
Under my feet,
In my bed.
Out the window,
Up the tree,
Down comes leaves
Onto the ground,
There again leaves
Are all around.

Kyle Dixon (9)
Ryhope Junior School, Sunderland

The Scary, Hairy Monster

The monster wore a Brownie costume.
He had 5 stinky, cheesy feet that smelt like a skunk.
It moved as slow as a tortoise.
He ate mouldy flies.
The monster had no table manners.
The monster was funny.
The monster had money,
So he bought some honey.

Holly Mclaughlin (9)
Ryhope Junior School, Sunderland

Summer

Summer comes
With birds whistling
Summer comes
With flowers blooming
Summer comes
With bees gliding
Summer comes
With pools shining
Summer comes
With alarm clocks ringing
Summer comes with me awaking, happy summer.

Luke Hammal (8)
Ryhope Junior School, Sunderland

Devil

D eadly demons come out at night.
E vil eagles scratch and give you a fright.
V ampires suck your blood.
I nvisible creatures scare you all night.
L urking lunatics walk round the streets.

Daniel Dunn (9)
Ryhope Junior School, Sunderland

Summer

Summer comes
   with hedgehogs walking.
Summer comes
   with people bathing.
Summer comes
   with birds tweeting.
Summer comes
   with animals grazing.
Summer comes
   with men relaxing.
Summer comes
   with women celebrating.
Summer comes to cheer me up.
Happy summer everyone.

Connor Usher (8)
Ryhope Junior School, Sunderland

Winter

The icy floor as the wind whistles
Through my hair.
The trees are dying
And I glide across the floor
The crunchy snow
And I sneeze
Through the breeze
The wind goes down the chimney pot
And goes through the house.
It goes into my room
And goes onto my toes
And the snow hides the world
Under the snow.

Brandon Lisle (8)
Ryhope Junior School, Sunderland

Summer Comes

Summer comes with the sun shining.
Summer comes with the sun blazing.
Summer comes with people bathing.
Summer comes with waves crashing.
Summer comes with water drinking.
Summer comes with dogs barking.
Summer comes with sausages popping.
Summer comes with people swimming.
Summer comes with birds singing.
Summer comes with flowers peeping.
Beautiful summer.

Zoe Knebel (8)
Ryhope Junior School, Sunderland

Snake

I slither through the grass like rope jelly.
Worm-slimy,
But fang-deadly.
Dressed in green zigs and black zags.
I hisssss.
My long tongue flicks in and out
Smelling my victim.
When I strike I bite.
Then squee-ee-ee-ze.
I'll crush you like an apple,
Then swallow you in one!
Gulp!
You're gone!

Shaun Broadley (10)
St Joseph's RC (VA) Primary School, Stanley

Cheetah

I am the racing car of the savannah
Wearing an expensive dress.
Teeth glinting with blood.
Legs bounding to my prey.
I pounce.
I bite.
My victim struggles but fails.
I taste the glorious tender meat.
Then vanish to find my next victim.

Steven Pendleton (10)
St Joseph's RC (VA) Primary School, Stanley

Gorilla

Swinging from tree to tree
I am king of the jungle
Crushing everything that gets in my way
Sitting on the top of my kingdom watching over my servants
Hunters trying to destroy my kingdom
I angrily beat my chest to prove I am king.

Adam Close (10)
St Joseph's RC (VA) Primary School, Stanley

Bat

I am the loudest screecher of the sky.
My fur is as black as coal.
My wings are leathery and jagged,
Swishing as I fly.
Hanging upside down in a dark and gloomy cave.
I'm waiting . . .
Hunting my prey at night-time,
I swoop from the air like a big black cannonball.
When I sleep I dream of a big, fat, juicy mouse.

Amy Sinclair (10)
St Joseph's RC (VA) Primary School, Stanley

Scorpion

I am the killer of the desert.
I murder with my stinger as sharp as a knife.
I am the mini tank of the sands.
My vicious pincers rip apart prey.
My jet-black armour is decorated with red tiger stripes.
I crash through jungles of termites unharmed.
I dream of attacking by surprise.

Stephen Cowan (11)
St Joseph's RC (VA) Primary School, Stanley

Lion!

I am the king of the jungle,
I am dressed in a rough, golden gown,
My sharp claws are digging into the hard, dirty ground,
I hide in the swishing grass as I spy on the victim,
Then I leap into the air and catch the innocent creature,
And bite into its delicate fur,
But it is too strong, it gets away with only a bite to spare,
I crawl home, furious and hungry,
I lie on my bed of soft fur and drift off into a deep sleep,
Dream of the delicious taste of blood.

Ashlee Richardson (10)
St Joseph's RC (VA) Primary School, Stanley

Slimy Slug!

Black slimy blob, lying like a lump of jelly,
Dressed in black rubber,
Slowly leaving a silvery, shining trail,
Struggling in and out of long green grass,
Careful, the gigantic long foot is coming.

Katie Rimington (10)
St Joseph's RC (VA) Primary School, Stanley

Tiger

I am the king of Africa,
I am dressed in yellow fur,
My legs help me move around and
My teeth help me catch my prey,
I dream that tomorrow I will get a
Big, juicy zebra.

Derek Weelands (10)
St Joseph's RC (VA) Primary School, Stanley

Lion's Den

My name is Leo
I am wrapped in gold fur
I hunt for my tea with my teeth
My favourite is zebra
Sshh, the zebra is close
I sprint, I pounce
I can't run as fast as a cheetah
I have got you now
'Teatime,' I roar
First I will rip the skin off, then eat everything
When I sleep I dream of my prey.

Christopher Pye (10)
St Joseph's RC (VA) Primary School, Stanley

Unicorn

I am a snow-white unicorn,
I will grant your wish and I'm friendly and trustworthy,
I trot between all the wildlife,
My magical horn sparkles day and night like diamonds,
I have a special friend that keeps me a secret,
When I sleep I dream of a unicorn friend.

Coral Brough (10)
St Joseph's RC (VA) Primary School, Stanley

Dog

I am yellow. A blonde dog,
Cuddly - a fat puppy dog,
Full of dog chocs and chew sticks,
My fur is as soft as a teddy bear's,
Shiny as polish,
I nip ears,
Bendy lobes and rubbery flaps,
I like to hug,
My paws on their shoulders,
My wet, pink tongue,
When I sleep,
I dream of fields,
Full of horse smells,
Cow smells,
Grass smells,
Smell smells!

Jonathon Hall (10)
St Joseph's RC (VA) Primary School, Stanley

The Tyrannosaurus Rex

I am the king of the lizards,
I wear a scaly robe,
My teeth are the size of tree stumps,
My claws are the size of *human legs,*
My favourite food is Iguanodon,
I spy on other dinosaurs,
Waiting . . . to pounce,
I make the kill!
As I eat,
I see some raptors stealing my eggs!
I run over but it's too late,
My eggs are gone!
As I sleep that night, I dream about killing egg-stealing velociraptors.

Brendan Faherty (10)
St Joseph's RC (VA) Primary School, Stanley

Rabbit

My name is Midnight,
Fluffy, white and furry, an ordinary rabbit!
Springing on the dew of the green grass,
Adorable I am, irresistible too,
I run fast and I'm bouncy,
I eat crunchy, hard carrots and delicious dandelion leaves.

Nicola Wall (10)
St Joseph's RC (VA) Primary School, Stanley

Shark

I am the most vicious fish of the deep blue sea,
My skin tough and solid like a battleship,
My teeth are as sharp as nails,
Stalking my prey I attack,
My fins flap wildly like a sharpened knife,
Everyone regrets to hear my name,
I am always alert for hunters,
When I sleep I dream of all the juicy, innocent fish I'll eat tomorrow.

Sean Waite (11)
St Joseph's RC (VA) Primary School, Stanley

Shark!

I am the big white shark
White as the clouds
I swim faster than a bullet
The bite!
I inflict pain on my opponent
I love the drip from my mouth
My skin so smooth, like leather
My teeth are as sharp as knives
My eyes are like black pebbles
My tail is like someone slapping you.

Lorenzo Fella (11)
St Joseph's RC (VA) Primary School, Stanley

The Eagle

I am the king of the evening sky,
Dressed in a golden gown of feathers.

My cragged claws clasp the branch of a tree,
My eyes are beady yellow slits.

I plunge and swoop through the air,
Gliding over the sleeping town.

Emma Donnelly (10)
St Joseph's RC (VA) Primary School, Stanley

The Monkey

I am the swinger of the jungle
I wear a dark brown fleece of fur
Swinging from tree to tree, branch to branch
Camouflaged in the trees
I shout out to my friends
'Ooo ooo, let's play!'
As we play the sun begins to set
'This is fun, but it's getting dark, I must go.'
As I sleep
I dream of playing with my friends the very next day.

Maxine Hamflett (11)
St Joseph's RC (VA) Primary School, Stanley

Gorilla

I'm the king of the treetops,
Dressed in a hairy black coat,
I'm as strong as a tank,
And I swing gracefully through the trees,
I'm the defender of the jungle,
Roaming in search of food.

Michael Handy (11)
St Joseph's RC (VA) Primary School, Stanley

The Eagle

I am the golden bird,
At night my eyes glitter in the darkness
At midday I see through the dazzle
That's when I swoop
Down
Like a missile
On target
I am the golden bird
Brilliant
Shining
When I sleep
I dream of the blue blank sky.

Chloe Costello (10)
St Joseph's RC (VA) Primary School, Stanley

Lion

My mane is strong
and dark as chocolate
I am king
of the yellow grass
and the warm slanting rocks.
I hunt the zebras
and the homed antelope
I camouflage in the grass.
I sleep
I dream of catching a rhino.

Aaron Waite (10)
St Joseph's RC (VA) Primary School, Stanley

The Peacock!

I am the gentle, soft, handsome bird.
I am dressed in a smooth colourful feather coat.
I leap and swoosh across the land
And dodge the huge green trees.
My colours look like a huge stained-glass window.
My eyes are as pretty as colourful marbles.
As I fall in a deep sleep,
I dream of my colours gleaming in the sun.

Megan Scott (10)
St Joseph's RC (VA) Primary School, Stanley

At Night

There's a whole new world in the midnight sky
The birds usually fly so high
Have gone to their lair
Their wings that flare so beautifully have run away
The fish have sunk into the depths of the deep blue sea
Have opened their homes with a magic key
Everywhere is sleeping. Is the world dead?

The trees that can whistle and blow
Have sunk, oh so low
The litter that rustles has been lost
There are no balls being tossed
Everywhere is sleeping. Is the world dead?
Is it only me who's awake?
Because I had a nightmare about a snake
Everyone in the world is dead
I wish I was instead!

Abbie Scarlett (11)
St Mary's RC Primary School, Sunderland

On A Sunny Afternoon

The sky is so bright
The birds take flight
All on a sunny afternoon

The owls they hoot
To a soothing flute
All on a sunny afternoon

As they await their delicious prey
The rats, the mice, in their burrow stay
All on a sunny afternoon

The trees are alive with life all around
With the whistling, rustling, crackling sound
All on a sunny afternoon

Oh how I like the sound of spring
And listen to the birds proudly sing
All on a sunny afternoon

Clear summer nights are almost here
The picnic season is so near
All on a sunny afternoon

The apples and oranges off the autumn floor
Accompanying the stones as the rivers pour
All on a sunny afternoon.

Abbie Kelf (10)
St Mary's RC Primary School, Sunderland

Love

Love is like a fire huddled up inside me.
Love is like a power holding me back.
Love is an urge screaming for freedom.
Love is my life holding me tender.
Love is like poetry swirling around.
Sometimes I don't know what love is.

Holly Raper (11)
St Mary's RC Primary School, Sunderland

The Big Match

It was the local derby Sunderland versus Newcastle
Getting to the ground, oh what a hassle
There were red and white and black and white shirts everywhere
All I could do was stand and stare
The players came out what a roar
All I wanted was for Newcastle to score
The game kicked off to a great cheer
Sunderland scoring was my biggest fear
Sunderland went charging for a goal
But to my delight Kevin Kyle fell down a hole
Newcastle got a corner the crowd roared
The Toon Army went barmy Newcastle scored
When the final whistle went, we had won 1-0
We all went home with a big smile, oh what a thrill.

Anthony Callaghan (9)
St Mary's RC Primary School, Sunderland

Stirring Spring

S pring is stirring very briskly
T ake a drink from your whisky
I love to watch all the flowers growing
R adiant daisies and daffodils blooming.
R alf, my dog's favourite thing is his ball,
I always have to get it, when it bounces over the wall,
N o more cold, no more snow,
G etting ready for the summer glow.

S how your little sister a fable
P ut some seeds into the bird table.
R ing the bells up in Heaven,
I t's my birthday and I am seven.
N ow just enjoy watching the beautiful things,
G o outside and feel the soft breeze spring.

Eszter Soos (10)
St Mary's RC Primary School, Sunderland

Raindrops

Pitter-patter
Pitter-patter
Rain falls through the sky
Trickle, gurgle
Trickle, gurgle
On the mountains high
Gurgling, babbling, gathering pace
Which little raindrop will win the race?
First a stream, then a brook
I wonder which way that first drop took
Down to the river, the raindrops go faster
Over the waterfall, oh now a disaster!
A roar so loud it would deafen you all
Faster and faster those raindrops fall
And just when they thought this is the end
They are at a lake that lurks just round the bend
So quiet, so still a beautiful place
Sunlight glistens on the surface
Hotter and hotter the sun shines down
The raindrops are rising but they don't know how!

Rebecca Adams (9)
St Mary's RC Primary School, Sunderland

Murder In The Country

When you're walking alone,
In the darkness of the deepest night,
That's when you will get the worst kind of fright.

Out of the shadows,
Comes a monstrous beast
Tearing up human flesh with his teeth.

Slitting throats with a knife
Pulling heads off with bare hands
So you better watch yourself
If you're walking alone at night.

Liam Walker (10)
St Mary's RC Primary School, Sunderland

Fun In The Snow

I woke up one morning to a carpet of snow,
Children were playing with faces aglow.
The sun was gone, the snow was here
And I knew at once some more would be near.

As night appeared the snow still lay
And I thought it would arrive again the next day,
The weather was crisp so I sat by the blaze,
So orangey and warm, so beautiful to gaze.

Later that night I was tucked up in bed,
With lovely thoughts running through my head,
I dreamt of the next day,
Which was not very far away.

I rushed downstairs with my coat and hat,
I went outside followed by my cat,
I went and played in the snow,
For tomorrow was all over, to school I would go.

Niamh Baldasera (10)
St Mary's RC Primary School, Sunderland

Dolphins

Dolphins dolphins they look at me
Dolphins dolphins they like me
Dolphins dolphins they swim through the sea
Just like me.

Dolphins always seem happy to me
They are always smiling as they swim through the sea
When they see me they smile at me
If they don't see me they are sad just like me.

Whenever I see them they play with me
Whenever I don't see them I feel alone
Whenever they swim underwater I am looking all over
When they pop up they give me a shock.

Simon French (9)
St Mary's RC Primary School, Sunderland

Skateboarding

I take my skateboard in the street
And down the path I glide
I balance carefully with my feet
And go into a lip slide.

I meet my friends at the park
And on he ramps we go
I slide the rail and make a spark
And get into the flow.

I move on to the half-pipe
And skate from side to side
I know I'm good at this type
Of skateboarding ride.

My friends and I we skate all day
At the skateboard park
An entry free we have to pay
And go home when it's dark.

Back through the streets on my board I go
Pushing with my feet
Feeling very tired and slow
Till I reach my door, dead beat!

Joseph Dunn (10)
St Mary's RC Primary School, Sunderland

Rain

R ain rain oh glorious rain
E veryone thinks you're a pain
S plishing and splashing
T hrough the street and down the drain

Sun

Sun sun oh wonderful sun
When you are out we have fun
Gloriously shining
Picnics for dining.

Anthony Lewis (9)
St Mary's RC Primary School, Sunderland

The Four Seasons

The early sun rises when spring is near, the birds they are tweeting
with such wonderful cheer
As rays of sunshine shines upon the lake, it's spring again
so it's good to be awake
Daffodils are blooming so yellow and bright, lots of pretty colour
in the sunlight.

Summer is here it's barbecue time, burgers and sausages,
swimming pools too, bicycles, tennis, there's lots to do!
Mum hang out the washing, T-shirts and shorts
and the sound of the ball on the tennis courts.
Everyone lying in the sun do they know autumn is about to come?

The crisp leaves are falling, golden and brown, the trees are swaying
and the wind makes us frown
Conker season is here; the children hang around the trees,
hitting them with sticks as they are falling in the breeze
The nip in the air is telling us soon winter will be here
Santa and reindeer!

The snow is falling, talk of Christmas cheer, sledges, snowmen
What can we hear?
Children talking of Santa excitement all around Christmas trees
And presents
Baby Jesus is crowned!
Another year is over and then you hear the sound,
New Year bells ringing all around!

Joshua Brown (11)
St Mary's RC Primary School, Sunderland

Squirrels

Squirrels jumping from tree to tree,
Hopping about and having their tea.
Squirrels' tails flying.
They're panting and sighing.
Squirrels, squirrels red and grey.
Always running, running away.

Kate Stenger (10)
St Mary's RC Primary School, Sunderland

The Three Bears

The mother bear, she cooked some gruel
Made from bits of rabbit and mule
But it was far too hot
'I'm burning my mouth!' said the little tot.
So they went for a walk on that warm sunny day
Not knowing what was coming their way
And up came greedy Goldilocks
Who before this smashed the car with rocks.
'I'm starving,' she said with an evil grin
And she went in the house, that's breaking in.
She tasted the porridge too cold, too hot
But the baby's was brill so she ate the whole pot.
Then she tried the chairs; too hard, too soft
But the baby's was brill. 'Fantastic,' she coughed
And squashed it flat like a piece of paper
And she fixed it using a stapler.
She didn't bother trying each bed
She just jumped into baby's and rested her head.
The bears came back and saw the state
The broken chair and the food off the plate.
They knew this was the handy work of the brat
So the bears on the door went rat-a-tat-tat.
So instead of eating the rest of the gruel
They ate Goldilocks and that was cruel!

Jessica Pye (10)
St Mary's RC Primary School, Sunderland

Summer

S ummer is the hottest thing
U nless it's raining
M e and my mates go out to play
M ore sun and time to play
E veryone is having fun
R un around lie on the ground
            because it's summer.

Craig MacDonald (9)
St Mary's RC Primary School, Sunderland

Cinderella

Here's what happened.
'Oh golly, oh heck,
I'd better run and save my neck!'
'Ho, ho now you're my groom to be,
So you must marry me!'
'I hope you don't mind,' she went on,
(By this time the prince wished she was gone)
'I have quite a bad blister . . .'
'That's not all you've got,' the prince said to the ugly sister.
An ugly face, with plenty of warts . . . I'm not marrying *you*,
I'll tell you who
I'm going to marry . .
I'll be happy if it isn't you,
For I'd rather marry Cinderella
(She thought he was a fine fella)
But . . .
He didn't and off he flew
And quickly flushed the offending shoe,
For a trip down the loo.

Ashleigh Simpson (9)
St Mary's RC Primary School, Sunderland

I Wonder

I wonder about the world we live in,
The trees we kill.
I wonder about the countries,
The creatures that thrive.
I wonder who I am,
What I will become.
I am who I am.
We are selfish,
Though it's never too late to change.

Rebecca Prestwood (11)
St Mary's RC Primary School, Sunderland

Toffee

I've got a hamster called Toffee
I really love him so
He's cute and cuddly
He's naughty and funny
I put him on my shoulder
And he climbs down my back
He loves fruit and veg
And he's mine all the time.

Melanie Golding (9)
St Mary's RC Primary School, Sunderland

Darkness

Deep into the dark of the stormy night
Is when I search for the light
I fight in no fear
Only knowing the monster is near

The time comes I have to fight
In the darkness of the night
The fear has struck me
Is he now going to kill me?

Matthew Harrison (10)
St Mary's RC Primary School, Sunderland

Beside The Sea

Breezy winds blowing in your face,
Soft sand tickling your feet,
Warm sea clear as can be,
Fish swimming calmly,
Crabs' legs moving cautiously,
Jellyfish stinging lots of lovely people,
Underwater mermaids swim playing hide-and-seek.

Rebecca Hughes (9)
St Mary's RC Primary School, Sunderland

My Poem

F rancesca is my name, football is my game
R ecorder is my fame
A ll you people out there are really just fine
N anna is all mine
C omputers make work so easy
E ducation can be so pleasing
S ports make me healthy
C herry drops are sweet and red
A pples are juicy and green

K elly is my second name
E ngland is where I live
L eaves are many colours
L ucky is my dog
Y ellow is my favourite colour.

Francesca Kelly (10)
St Mary's RC Primary School, Sunderland

Clouds In Many Shapes

Clouds form in many shapes,
Like faces, dragons, dogs, cars and cats
But most times just fluff.
Some people think that one cloud
Is a ghost and other people think that
The same cloud is a face.
Sometimes most of the clouds
Are joined together so that they make
Just one big cloud.
It doesn't make a shape at all.
Clouds will always be fluffy like cotton wool.

Emily Bird (9)
St Mary's RC Primary School, Sunderland

Night

Darkness wrapped around me,
Like a blanket of blackness it silently crept.
It started to come and surround me,
Like a fearless lion onto me it leapt.

It is a giant shadow
Which is watching, following me everywhere.
It hides up above and down below,
Waiting to kidnap me into its lair.

It descends on the people that it meets,
Concealing them in an ebony cloak.
Covering houses, trees and streets,
It drifts along like pitch-black smoke.

Then from the silence, sounds can be heard,
The howl of a wolf from the wood.
And from the blackness, the cry of a bird,
These noises are not understood.

From behind the clouds drifts the full moon,
Highlighting the ripples on a moonlit lake.
The wind whistles its mournful tune,
Winding round houses like a sinister snake.

Beware of the night-time,
It has not one fear,
But when it sees light
It will all disappear.

Lizzie Fetherston (11)
St Mary's RC Primary School, Sunderland

The Fish Wish

Once I caught a fish
It said, 'Set me free please
Do not have me for your tea.'
I let him go and he laughed at me.
The next day I caught him again for my tea.

Bret McCarthy (10)
St Mary's RC Primary School, Sunderland

A Paper Aeroplane

I fly my paper aeroplane up into the sky,
It looks like a rocket flying higher and higher
It starts to come down
But before it can land,
I fly another aeroplane up
Into the sky flying higher and higher.

Jason Gray (9)
St Mary's RC Primary School, Sunderland

Sea Storm

Spray leaping over the drenched pier,
A ship in distress is the sound I hear,
Thunder clashes, lightning strikes,
This is a storm that nobody likes.
'Help me! Help me!' the captain is calling,
While into the water his sailors are falling.
The sea gods are angry, they're starting a storm,
But inside the cottage it's cosy and warm.
The people are worried, it's a storm they've never seen,
But the captain of the ship hopes it's all a big dream.
Though he knows it is not, he will drown very soon,
But he's going to Heaven to watch over you.

Lucy Farrell (10)
St Mary's RC Primary School, Sunderland

Buttons

There once was a horse called Buttons.
He was brown and white with eyes so bright.
Big and strong with a mane so long,
That was the horse called Buttons.
He could jump so high,
Almost touched the sky,
At times he thought that he could fly.

Sophie Fenwick (10)
St Mary's RC Primary School, Sunderland

The Rules Of Football

The rules of football are
If a player is fouled bad
The referee will be very mad.
He will say no dirty tackles lad,
If strikers always score goals,
Managers make their contracts roll.
The man in black's a lonely figure,
His finger's always on the trigger of decisions.
No matter what he's always right,
I don't know how he sleeps at night.
Managers always making a dash
To buy new players with their cash.
This football thing is a funny game,
It's enough to drive us all insane.
At full time the ref gives a toot,
Then all the players hang up their boots.

Cameron Phillips (10)
St Mary's RC Primary School, Sunderland

April

In April when the forest sways
Are all made sweet
With roses and violets
New opened at your feet.
Look up and see a beautiful tree
With blossom white
And branches on trees so slender.
When I saw the pink leaves
Looking tender.
I saw that beautiful tree
Such a lovely thing to see.

Laila Mahmoodshahi (10)
St Mary's RC Primary School, Sunderland

United Swords

Fighting begins on this faithful day
The crew are armed, attack when they may.
A ring of laughter could be heard
As the two ships clashed in combat.

Blood is dripping all around
The shouts and yells a dreadful sound
But one man stands alive alone
Upon the rundown ship.

The name of he was Captain Done
And on this ship he always won
The battle that was in his way
Upon United Swords.

Holly Smith (9)
St Mary's RC Primary School, Sunderland

Weather

Sometimes it rains
Sometimes it snows
That makes it cold

Then again it could be . . .
Warm and sunny
That is nice

My favourite weather is
Sun and snow
Snow is white and fluffy
Sun is hot and warm all day

That's why I like weather.

Georgina Currie (10)
St Mary's RC Primary School, Sunderland

A Winter Day

One cold morning, when I woke up,
I opened my curtain and took a look.
Everything was covered in a white carpet.

Icicles that made me stop and stare,
Had formed on rooftops everywhere.

Snowflakes fell from the sky like powder,
As the children sang carols louder.

The trees had a sprinkle of white dust on them,
I heard the crinkle of the snow when a car went past.

I saw smoke drifting into the sky from the chimneys.
A woman shifted the snow from her drive.
The sun slowly pushed into the sky.
How long will the snow lie?

Matthew Barber (10)
St Mary's RC Primary School, Sunderland

Candy Sweet

C louds look like candyfloss floating in the air
A pples come in green and red and can be used in crumble and pie
N ectar is what bees collect from the flowers in the spring
D affodils appear in your garden, what a beautiful thing
Y achts go sailing on the sea in the summer breeze

S taying at Gran's is brilliant and I never want to leave
W illy Wonka has a factory that makes lots of sweets
E ating them is so much fun, I get them as treats
E aster is the time of year where you go to church to pray and sing
T o go to this school I think is a wonderful thing.

Katherine Lamb (10)
St Mary's RC Primary School, Sunderland

Tiger

Tiger, tiger eyes so bright
They even glow in the night.

He crawls and stalks
Across the ground,
With sense of smell
As strong as a hound.

That mighty tiger men have seen,
With a coat that glows with a mighty beam.
With a speed of foot
Second to none
That mighty tiger
Has come and gone.

Josh Kelly (9)
St Mary's RC Primary School, Sunderland

Rain!

Rain, rain
How I do like it to rain
And I watch the flowers grow,
As they take in all that water
From all that soggy soil!

Rain, rain
How I do love the rain
And I watch the clouds disappear
I start to feel sad
That it won't rain again.

Rain, rain, rain!

Sarah Forrest (10)
St Mary's RC Primary School, Sunderland

Horse

Some horses gallop wild and free
Some horses don't and get ridden by me.

Some get groomed so their coats are glossy
Some of them don't and get really grotty.

Some are kept in airy stables
Some of them graze in lush green fields.

But pony, stallion, mare or foal I don't care
I love them all!

Christie Bainbridge (10)
St Mary's RC Primary School, Sunderland

One Winter's Day

It was one winter's day
The snow was bright as a light
We went up all the mountains
And slipped down on the ice
We ran across the rivers
Ran across the seas
Until we went home to have our tea.

Matthew Banks (10)
St Mary's RC Primary School, Sunderland

Spring

Springtime has come at last
The flowers are starting to rise
As more babies are born tonight
From the love of Jesus Christ

As the blistering, beaming sun appears
Little animals too
I do grow as well
With my younger brother too!

Caitlin Hindmarsh (9)
St Mary's RC Primary School, Sunderland

Cinderella

Cinderella had such a life,
Her dad had gone and left his wife.
It wasn't just her he left behind,
He had two step-daughters, who were unkind.
Every day she'd cook and clean,
The ugly sisters were so mean.
Cinderella had a heart of gold,
The other two were spotty and old.
The prince's butler came to the door,
But he couldn't believe what he saw.
'An invitation for you all,
To enjoy the prince's ball!'
'We'd love you to come,' said the terrible two
'But tonight's the night to clean the loo!'
So off they went, the two old dears,
Leaving poor Cinders, at home in tears.
The fairy godmother arrived in a puff of smoke,
'I will help you and that's no joke!
You will have a carriage with horses,
That are good prancers,
Then to the ball you'll go for all the dances.
She was the prettiest woman at the ball,
The prince was waiting to meet her in the hall.
When he saw her his heart missed a beat,
The prince couldn't resist,
Whisking her off her feet!

Rebecca Smith (9)
St Mary's RC Primary School, Sunderland

A Poem About Wind

The wind is the breath of a giant.
It storms through trees.
Whirling leaves
Cartwheeling through the cold air.

Waves crashing against the cliffs angrily.
Seagulls struggling through the stormy sky
Bend backwards.

The washing line shakes madly
Clothes like acrobats do tumble turns.
Falling and flapping in the booming air.

William Lewis (9)
St Mary's RC Primary School, Sunderland

What Is Blue?

Blue is a flower
On the grass,
It needs a shower
From a glass.
Blue is a monster
In the house,
It pops out of a lobster
Like a mouse.
Blue is a book
With lots of pages,
I have a hook
And lots of cages.
Blue is a top
Nice and soft
When you drop it
It goes plop
From the loft.

Alex Tang (7)
St Patrick's RC Primary School, Ryhope

What Is Blue?

Blue is paint that has been splashed on the wall
All through the day
To make a ball.
Blue is eyes that
Blink in fright,
Blue is a monster
That jumps out in the night.
Blue is a bluebell
In the garden,
Blue is a coat
With a word saying pardon,
Blue is wallpaper
That is stuck on the wall,
Blue is the most powerful
Colour of all.
Blue is a list
That I have lost,
Blue is the sky
In the mist.

Charlie Addison (7)
St Patrick's RC Primary School, Ryhope

The Tiger

The tiger lifts its big paw
And then it pokes out its long claw.

The tiger pounces on its prey,
Hoping to catch some food today.

The tiger jumped so high,
It nearly touched the sky.

The tiger plays on a cliff,
With its friend who's called Sniff.

Louise Gardiner (9)
St William's RCVA Primary School, Trimdon Village

Rabbits

Twitching nose,
Furry toes,

Fluffy feet,
Small heartbeat,
Lots of crunchy carrots to eat.

Tiny paws,
Sleeps on straw,
I really love cute rabbits,
Even when they chew plants to bits.

Floppy ears,
Claws like spears.

Eating grass,
As they pass.

Gleaming eyes
Giving you a surprise!

Olivia Dowling (8)
St William's RCVA Primary School, Trimdon Village

Dog In The Corner

A dog so sweet in the corner
Lying down her name is Lorna
I shouted her name
She still was lying down the same.

Somebody came to the door
She used to bark in galore
She used to be mad
But now she looks so sad.

She used to play out in the sun
With a little soft bun
I love her so much
She was such a soft touch.

Jane Snowball (8)
St William's RCVA Primary School, Trimdon Village

Family Food

My mother gave me egg on toast,
This is what I like the most,
My father gave me horses' liver,
It made me shake, it made me shiver,
My sister gave me six green peas,
But whoops I drooped them on my knees,
My brother gave me rotten beans,
Horrid, horrid's what it means,
My best friend gave me a hairy sweet,
Because he saw my massive feet,
My teacher gave me stinky pie,
But extra homework is no lie,
My cousin gave me baccy to smoke,
I did, I stopped, it made me choke,
My auntie Sam she gave me lunch,
Well actually it's more like brunch,
My auntie Sam she made it lush,
And now my tum's the size of a bush,
But now my family are in a huff,
Because their meals I'd had enough,
I was locked up into room,
Full of grief and full of gloom,
So this is the end of my happy life,
I won't ever touch another fork or knife,
I'll see you later, well I hope.

Sarah Hawley (10)
St William's RCVA Primary School, Trimdon Village

Babies

B abies are cute
A dults adore them
B abies cry
 I f you don't like them waking up
E specially in the night
S ometimes all they do is sleep.

Shannon Turnbull (9)
St William's RCVA Primary School, Trimdon Village

What A Dragon Is Like

There once was a dragon
That had fire like charcoal.

His eyes were like pebbles
On the seashore.

His legs are like brick
Fortresses on hard rock.

His tail was like a butcher's
Knife swiping on meat.

His head was like
a metal pole.

His heart pounds like
snow falling into an avalanche.

His teeth are like
a bunch of teenagers chatting.

Now you know that you
do not want to meet a dragon!

Robert Moran (9)
St William's RCVA Primary School, Trimdon Village

Santa Poem

S o silent at night
A lways gives presents
N ever misses a house
T o bring joy to all
A ll silent in bed

C onsiderate to all
L ove and happiness
A lways never gets caught
U npacks presents
S anta's his name.

Tom Robertshaw (9)
St William's RCVA Primary School, Trimdon Village

A Fairy's Life

There was a young fairy with wings of gold,
Any lie she never told,
Her hair shone in the moonlight,
She was so beautiful what a nice sight,
Her mother gave her the gift of grace,
Her father gave her a dress made of lace,
Last week she was due to marry,
A dazzling boy named Prince Barry,
At the altar he nearly did faint,
He said his wife looked like a saint,
Her wedding ring was a big red ruby,
Her dress was made by designer Duby,
As they stepped into the wooden carriage,
Barry said, 'I really love marriage.'
Two years later they had a kid,
It was a boy they called him Sid.
One month later they had another child,
This one they didn't want because he was wild.
Mrs Mary the kind fairy
And Mr Barry who she did marry and little Sid too,
Moved to a place in Scotland called Pear
And no more about them we did hear.

Rachael Donnachie (10)
St William's RCVA Primary School, Trimdon Village

Babies

B eautiful, elegant things
A lot of time needed
B ig responsibility
I   n need of lots of love
E very day
S pecial to you and Mummy too.

Claire Harnett (9)
St William's RCVA Primary School, Trimdon Village

Me And My Friends

Samantha is so brainy,
Samantha is so kind,
You can call her strange
And she won't even mind.

Rachael is so dazzling,
Rachael is so loud,
She jumps about, she screams and shouts
And she always attracts a crowd.

Sarah is so jolly,
Sarah is so sweet,
She always has a lolly,
She eats them with her feet.

Adam is so small,
Adam is so mad,
His mouth is so tall,
It makes up for it all.

All my friends together,
We are so very clever,
Especially Sam,
She's the head of our gang.

Emily Ruth Lovett (11)
St William's RCVA Primary School, Trimdon Village

Horse Poem

H orses galloping through the night
O r it's a wonderful sight
R iding horses by and by
S eeing the magic from the horse's world
E ating apples everyday
S ee the moonlight of the horses blow away.

Kate Hewitt (8)
St William's RCVA Primary School, Trimdon Village

Down The Path

As I walked down the path
I saw a tree, I saw a tree
That was looking at me.

As I walked down the path
I saw a dog, oh what a creature
Not like a frog

As I walked down the path
I saw a rat running up a tree
Oh it was so fat

As I walked down the path
I saw my friends having a laugh
Because I had two odd socks on
And that's the end.

Stephanie Storey (11)
St William's RCVA Primary School, Trimdon Village

Cats

Cats! Cats! Cats!
They always lie on mats.

Mostly in the sun,
They don't normally go for a run.

They all have nine lives,
Don't ever hang around beehives.

When they have kittens,
They are as soft as mittens.

They always eat more than an ounce
And they do a really big pounce.

Nicole Peters (9)
St William's RCVA Primary School, Trimdon Village

My Crazy Family

Welcome to my house,
I think you will agree,
We are a crazy family . . .

Mum is so busy,
She works round and round,
Her feet don't touch the ground . . .

Next is my super dad,
He works hard all day,
He says goodbye to all his pals
And comes home for a little play . . .

Now there is the children,
I don't think she should go there,
They are wild like a grisly bear.

Sophie Fellows (8)
St William's RCVA Primary School, Trimdon Village

If I Was Famous

If I was famous,
I'd be loaded with money,
I would have for breakfast,
Delicious bread and honey.

If I was famous,
I'd have designer clothes,
A little pink sleeveless top
And lipstick as red as a rose.

If I was famous
I'd sing very sweetly,
I'd put my make-up on,
Ever so neatly.

Grace Robinson (9)
St William's RCVA Primary School, Trimdon Village

My Little Sister Em

My little sister Emily is the cutest thing.
She can walk, talk and she can sing.

She loves Bob the Builder, she has him on video.
She also loves Scooby Doo, eh I don't know.

On Hallowe'en she dressed up as the Devil,
She looked so devious she made me tremble.

We ask her who is the best football team,
'Chelsea,' she shouts with a little scream.

When we leave to go back to Mam's house
She cries and cries like a little mouse.

Em's normally plays with her babies and Bob
Except when she's upset she starts to sob.

Annabel May Hill (10)
St William's RCVA Primary School, Trimdon Village

If I Was . . .

If I was a pop star,
I'd be Britney Spears,
But I'm an elephant with great big ears.

If I was an author,
I'd be J K Rowling,
Instead I'm a bear that never stops growling.

If I was a celebrity,
I'd be Ant or Dec,
But now I'm a giraffe with a very long neck.

Courtney Sheen (9)
St William's RCVA Primary School, Trimdon Village

The Killer

The shadow moves as smooth as silk,
The door is left ajar.
You tiptoe in the room. 'Who's there?'
Duck down ever so far.

The coast is clear, set off again,
The family's gone to bed.
Snatch the gun from your pocket,
Blast them in the head.

Sirens are heard, you're in a rush,
You feel guilty and mad.
Police burst in and you are caught,
These murderers are bad.

You plead for mercy, it doesn't work.
You're drowned by the sound of cars.
You are pulled out, they slam the door.
Now you're trapped behind bars.

Timothy Jasper (10)
St William's RCVA Primary School, Trimdon Village

Going Back 110,000 Years Ago

This little ditty
Begins 110,000 years ago
Just as it began to snow
Down with the dinosaurs heading for cover
The water froze a metre thick
Topped off with snow
'It is the age of the ice!'
Cried the dinosaurs
It lasted for 100 years
But at last it started to thaw
Spring was here at last, at last!

Ashley Francis (10)
St William's RCVA Primary School, Trimdon Village

The Flower Crime

One day the cops came after me
I was frightened out of my pants
I only stole a couple of massive sunflower plants
I got them from the florist
And that is when they came
Well, I know who's to blame
I got locked in a cell for a month or two
Now I know, never what to do.

Dominic Trotter (9)
St William's RCVA Primary School, Trimdon Village

Flying High

Hello there I am Lucy Loo,
I wish this poem wasn't true,
I floated inside a bubble,
That was the cause of all my trouble.
My sister blew it so high,
I started to fly
And over the treetops I went.

Hello there I am Lucy Loo,
I wish this poem wasn't true,
I saw the people on the ground
And all of a sudden there was a loud sound,
There in front of me was an aeroplane
Air Jet was its name
And over the house tops I went.

Hello there I am Lucy Loo,
I wish this poem wasn't true,
I went over my large school,
And I popped on the chimney top,
I landed straight into the pool,
As I climbed out I was trying to look cool,
Miss Wobble said, 'Late again Miss Loo.'

Danielle Palmer & Catherine Head (11)
The Links Primary School, Stockton-on-Tees

The Nebbles

The Nebbles make a happy home,
In seaside town of Gandyome.
They feed on sand and live in rocks
And sleep on leaves and smelly socks.
Now one day they found a pebble,
What an adventure for the Nebbles!

Nebbles, Nebbles what a sight!
Always jolly, always bright!

The pebble talked about his life
And how back home he had a wife.
He talked about his kids and pets
And how he used to place his bets.
His favourite crab was 'Run-along-faster',
Unfortunately, it was a complete disaster!

Nebbles, Nebbles what a sight!
Always jolly, always bright!

One day that pebble ran away,
To a place called 'Farraday'.
The Nebbles chased it, running fast,
Till they caught it with a net, at last.
And now they live in harmony,
The Nebbles and the pebbles on the beach.

Nebbles, Nebbles what a sight!
Always jolly, always bright!

Alex Seymour & Catriona Bruce (10)
The Links Primary School, Stockton-on-Tees

The Animals

I am the eagle looking for my prey.
I am the shark looking for my match
And I am the kangaroo boxing my head off.
We are the animals looking for our food.

Edward Batley (8)
The Links Primary School, Stockton-on-Tees

The Ajbaz

The Ajbaz were dreaming of Africa,
On a cold and windy day,
They were thinking how to travel there,
When a gusty wind came their way,
Suddenly they were up in the air
And carried on without a care.
On a dandelion clock they flew,
From Roseberry Topping to Africa,
They flew, they flew, they flew!

They were travelling at sixty mph,
Flying so high on their clock,
Across the land and over the sea,
They came to an African dock,
By now they were hoping to land,
But all they could see was sand.
On a dandelion clock they flew,
From Roseberry Topping to Africa,
They flew, they flew, they flew!

Ben Quinn (10) & Emma Bonnard (11)
The Links Primary School, Stockton-on-Tees

Roller Coaster Ride

First you climb to the sun,
But that isn't the only fun.
The last climb takes a long time.
What a height,
It's a wonderful sight!
But wait, have a rest,
Because here is the best.
I feel like I'm going to die!
But now you can have a sigh,
Because that is the end of the roller coaster ride.

Joe Bostock-Jones (9)
The Links Primary School, Stockton-on-Tees

Alphabet Poem

A is for ant very tiny and small,
B is for bat that doesn't fly at day,
C is for crawling all over the place,
And D is for 'drat'! 'I don't know my way.'

E is for empty, cold and damp,
F is for fat, so they can't put their top on,
G is for giraffe, so tall and thin
And H is for hat but now there's none.

I is for ice, frozen and hard,
J is for jump, right into the air,
K is for kick, when you're in karate,
and L is for lump so high and rare.

M is for monkey that swings on the trees,
N is for nose that grows on your face,
O is for octopus, with lots of legs,
and P is for pose, they do look ace.

Q is for quill, that are all gone now,
R is for race so, run really fast,
S is for sun, that shines nice and bright,
And T is for trace, and I've drawn a cast.

U is for umbrella, that's very colourful,
V is for violin, that plays lovely tunes,
W is for water, so crystal clear,
X is for X-ray, that doctors use,
Y is for you that everyone likes
And Z is for zebra that says 'bye bye!'

Thomas Donald (9)
The Links Primary School, Stockton-on-Tees

Umpa-Lumpa

Umpa-Lumpa I found you up my jumpa,
Now you live in a jam jar,
In my garage on my car bumpa,
You are driven to the bar,
In my ma's car,
You are small and creepy -
Tall and leapy!

Then at night you creep into my room,
You read my books
And ruin my project of a tomb,
You say you can cook,
While giving me a scary look,
You are small and leapy -
Tall and creepy!

One happy day,
We went to school,
All happy with a fulfilled play,
And out you slipped in my drool,
Out you leapt onto the head of the boy, who was cool,
You are small and creepy -
Tall and leapy!

You itch and scratch,
Making him run, cry and scream,
In a bath-filled-dream,
You are small and creepy -
Tall and leapy!

Beccy Tait (11) & Bethany Dodd (10)
The Links Primary School, Stockton-on-Tees

My Friend

My friend is cool,
He sits on a stool.
In the morning,
He is boring.
In the afternoon,
He is a baboon.
In the night,
He is bright.
But at mid morning,
He is snoring.

Helen Douglas (9)
The Links Primary School, Stockton-on-Tees

My Life

My life is boring,
It's like my aunt's lad snoring.
People say I look like a fool,
I wish I looked like Nicky Cool.
My best friend is my family,
Because they spoil me.

Liam Kendrick
The Links Primary School, Stockton-on-Tees

Books

Books, books,
They get you in hooks.
Why do we have them in school?
Because they are so exciting and cool.
Some are big, some are small,
Some are as big as a mall.

Daniel Addis (8)
The Links Primary School, Stockton-on-Tees

Astro Platypus

There once was a platypus called Ben,
Who went to the moon on a hen,
As he landed on the moon,
He heard a funny tune
And this became number one for Ben.

A Martian came marching along,
Who was playing ping-pong,
With his friend, Zuffong,
Singing their favourite song,
Which became number one for Ben.

They had a visit to Mars,
Looking at their favourite stars,
They took off in their rocket ship,
Then did an amazing flip,
Which became number one for Ben.

Jack Chaytor (11) & Wasif Syed (10)
The Links Primary School, Stockton-on-Tees

Seasons

In winter you will sneeze,
But be careful not to freeze.
I'm happy in spring, as bells ring.
You can look at the stars
And hear the passing cars.
In the summer sun,
You can run and run.
In autumn it's winter soon,
So view the lovely moon.
Spring, summer, autumn, winter,
They are all great.
There indeed, is a need,
To celebrate.

Katie Brooks (9)
The Links Primary School, Stockton-on-Tees

The Gummies

We tried to fly to the sun we did,
We tried to fly to the sun.
Our friends said we were dumb they did,
Our friends said we were dumb.
Our little snowflake nearly melted,
But we quickly got away.
It hurt we crashed,
We boomed and bashed,
We landed in Bombay.

Far away, far away
Are the lands where the Gummies play.
They're pink and orange,
Gold and grey,
A new adventure every day!

We were still determined to fly we were,
We were still determined to fly.
We stopped at the local café we did,
We stopped for an apple pie.
Also at the café,
We bought some bright pink taffy,
It was sticky and nice,
Because we added some spice.

Far away, far away
Are the lands where the Gummies play,
They're pink and orange,
Gold and grey,
A new adventure every day!

The wind came blowing,
The sky came snowing,
We drifted away
For half a day.
We were almost there,
When we snacked on a pear.
We were rather close,
Not like us to boast.

Far away, far away
Are the lands where the Gummies play,
They're pink and orange,
Gold and grey,
A new adventure every day!

We nearly got to the sun we did,
We nearly got to the sun.
Our little snowflake turned to water,
It wasn't very much fun.

Far away, far away
Are the lands where the Gummies play,
They're pink and orange,
Gold and grey,
A new adventure every day!

Laura Elsdon & Leanne Skipper (10)
The Links Primary School, Stockton-on-Tees

My Dog

My dog loves to play
But she always gets mucky
So she has a bath
She is
Cute
Cuddly
Soft
Brown
Funny
And she has blue eyes
With a black nose that is soft
Ears are droopy and soft.

Rachel Walker (8)
The Links Primary School, Stockton-on-Tees

My Rocket Ship

If I was an astronaut I would
F
l
y
To the Milky Way
And land in my
White chocolate-shaped
Rocket ship.

Laura Douglas (9)
The Links Primary School, Stockton-on-Tees

A Day At School

Maths in the morning,
Assembly is pretty boring.
After that it's playtime,
In literacy we have to do a rhyme.
Science is number 1,
Lunchtime is really fun.
ICT hip hip hooray,
Hometime at the end of the day.
Now it's time to go out and play.

Matthew Bone (8)
The Links Primary School, Stockton-on-Tees

I Hate Poems

Oh I hate poems
They're such a drag
They're such boring things
So what is the point?
They're such a waste of time
So why are we doing this?
Why? Teacher why?

Jacob Bulmer (9)
The Links Primary School, Stockton-on-Tees

Song Of The Animal World

The dog goes . . . woof!
The cat goes . . . *miaow!*
The crab goes . . . snap!

Bark at the girl
Bark at the boy
And being a dog
Barking is my job

Take a long nap
Take a long sleep
Open one eye
And have a little peep

Snip over here
Snap over there
Snip at the fish
Snap everywhere.

Francesca Cosstick (8)
The Links Primary School, Stockton-on-Tees

A World Of Fantasy

Witches and wizards
Fighting with magic
Goblins and elves
Working for their keep
Pegasus the flying horse
Spending his time in the night sky
Dragons and fairies
Want to get their own way
Happy am I when meeting them
In a world of fantasy!

Katie Hannah Peeling (9)
The Links Primary School, Stockton-on-Tees

Loving Your Family

F rom small to big,
A family is for loving,
M ums are always there for you
 I have a dad who is kind too
L ucy is my sister I love her so so much
Y our family loves you whichever way you look!

Megan Bunford (9)
The Links Primary School, Stockton-on-Tees

Fairy Folk

If you go down to the bottom of my garden
Where I play,
You will see the fairy folk
Till the end of the day.
Play with them and they'll play with you.
A little twinkle, a little peek,
See their magic, it's strong not weak.
Colours, glitter and a sigh of happiness.

You'll very soon see
What I mean by fairy folk!

Emily Bostock-Jones (9)
The Links Primary School, Stockton-on-Tees

Theme Park

When we go in the sun,
We will go and have some fun.
When we go in the rain,
We will go on the ghost train.

When we go on the coconut shy,
I see a ride that's really high.
Some rides are really fast,
That's why I go on them last.

Matthew Rossiter (9)
The Links Primary School, Stockton-on-Tees

I Met

I met a cat as I went walking;
We got talking,
Cat and I.
'Where are you going to Cat?' I said
I said to the cat as he went by,
'Down to the farm to get some mice.
Will you come with me?'
'No not I.'

I met a lion as I was walking;
We got talking,
Lion and I.
'Where are you going to Lion,' I said
I said to Lion as he went by
Down to the zoo to get some meat
'Will you come with me?'
'No not I.'
'Where are you going to Lion?' I said
I said to Lion as he went by
Down to the zoo to get some meat,
'Will you come with me?'
'Not I.'

Courtney Howgill (7)
The Links Primary School, Stockton-on-Tees

My Cat

I love my cat because she's . . .
cute,
cuddly,
funny,
black,
small,
friendly
and playful
and I love her wiggly tail!

Katy Longstaff (9)
The Links Primary School, Stockton-on-Tees

One Love

You can only have one love in the world
One love in the world
There are many fish in the sea
You know what I mean
But there is one special one for you and me
Then you see that your hate may melt
And that special one might be me.

Danielle Hislop (7)
The Links Primary School, Stockton-on-Tees

When The Alien Came To Tea

When the alien came to tea,
It was a grand sight to see.
Six big googly eyes were staring straight at me.
I took him into my house
And sat him in front of the TV.
There was rock 'n' roll that night,
When the alien came to tea.
I offered him some sponge cake,
With strawberries and cream.
He whipped them up and smiled
And said, 'We make a great team!'

Helen Greenough (8)
The Links Primary School, Stockton-on-Tees

My Dog

My dog is happy
My dog is fun
My dog she likes to run run run.

Her name is Megan
Her friend is scruff
And when they play it's rough rough rough.

Ashleigh Collins (8)
The Links Primary School, Stockton-on-Tees

Poem To Perform

I met a pig, we went walking
We went talking
Pig and I
'Where are you going?' I said
(To pig as she went walking by)
'Down to the town of course to get some pig food,' said pig
'Will you come with me?'
'No not I.'

Ashleigh McWilliams (8)
The Links Primary School, Stockton-on-Tees

Roller Coaster

A roller coaster, a roller coaster ride,
It's so big, it stands with pride.
It's fast and scary,
It leaves me feeling wary.
I'm feeling sick, too much food
That I have chewed.
It's speeding along the track,
All the way back
To where the ride started.

Patrick Geldard-Williams (9)
The Links Primary School, Stockton-on-Tees

Chip The Magic Otter

Chip the magic otter
Lives in the sea
He dives in the water
And looks for his tea
He twirls around and does tricks
All around the sea
Chip wallops through the water
And kicks his enemy.

Sally Fox (8)
The Links Primary School, Stockton-on-Tees

Song Of The Animal World

The monkey goes . . . chita chata
The lion goes . . . roar
The snake goes . . . sss

I climb tree to tree
I can be very cheeky
I can be good, I can be bad
But me monkey is very bad.

Everything lives, everything dares, everything roars
The monkey . . . chita chata
The lion . . . roar
The snake . . . sss

I am king of the forest
I roar, I eat, I drink
I eat animals, I am king of the forest.

Everything lives, everything roars
The monkey . . . chita chata
The lion . . . roar
The snake . . . sss

I'm the snake that slithers
Through the leaves and round
Round the trees
I go under the leaves
And up the trees

Everything lives, everything dances, everything roars
The monkey . . . chita chata
The lion . . . roar
The snake . . . sss.

Tonicha Clarke (8)
The Links Primary School, Stockton-on-Tees

A Salty Poem

Have you seen the waves of the sea
Crashing on the rocks?
Washing up shells,
But did you go deeper?
Deeper into the stormy water
To visit a watery mermaid princess
In her salt bed where the fishes pass
With a splish splash, hear a roar
And a moan and a groan
And you look to a flashing city
As you remember the slippery kiss
As the sun goes down.

Faye Wilson (7)
The Links Primary School, Stockton-on-Tees

Tudors

Tudors poor
Tudors rich
Tudors digging in a ditch
Tudors cooking round a pot
Tudors feeling very hot
Tudors sleeping
Tudors snoring
Tudors being very boring.

Alana Senior (8)
The Links Primary School, Stockton-on-Tees

Big Elf's Sweet Land!

Deep inside a sweet shop,
Running on a shelf,
Lies a little creature
And his name is Elf.
He soars on a jelly bean,
Searching for a sweet,
He spots a sherbet bon-bon
And then begins to eat.
Little Elf, little Elf,
Eat more sweets,
You will grow bigger
When you start to eat!

You have grown big ears,
So fly far away,
To a land where there are sweets
And you can eat all day.
You have reached the island,
Eat, eat and eat,
It will be quite tasty
And an enjoyable treat!
Little Elf, little Elf,
Eat more sweets,
You will grow bigger,
When you start to eat!

Gummy Bears, sugar worms
And much, much more,
Marshmallows, Haribos,
That you so adore,
Sweet land, sweet land,
Yum, yum, yum,
Sour and sweet,
Good for your tum.
Big Elf, big Elf,
No more sweets,
You have grown bigger,
Because you started to eat.

Jenny Openshaw (10) Sarah Bonnard & Sarah Brown (11)
The Links Primary School, Stockton-on-Tees

Peter Pan

For all there's Wendy dear,
Her father does drink beer.
She lives with her family now,
They don't milk any kind of cow.
All this is how it began,
Now Peter Pan is a different man.
Peter Pan can fly
Look there! He's in the sky.
Tinkerbell is a pixie
Don't be mean because she's titchy,
They all flew off to Neverland,
They never came back to England.

Danielle Louise Steel (10)
Witherwack Primary School, Sunderland

The Horrible Witch

Her broomstick goes under he legs
Oh! She doesn't like pegs

She has a black cat
And she's always eating dead rats
And she likes bats

She's got black eyes
And she's always telling lies
And she's always eating ice cream pies

She will shout at you and scare you
And her house is like doom.

Amy Leadbitter (8)
Wiitherwack Primary School, Sunderland

This Place Is A Creep

Remember goblins live alone,
Remember this is a scary poem.
When one's glimpse into eyes,
Add to the cauldron some
Old shaggy flies.
Remember broomsticks,
Rags and hats.
Witches fly around with
Old shaggy cats.

Remember the hook,
Remember the pain.
Say goodbye to the skeletons
On the train.
By golly, this place is a creep,
Remember monsters
Lurk and peep.
If you go to the castle at night,
You will get a surprising fright.

James Stoddart (8)
Wiitherwack Primary School, Sunderland

Witches

Witches think they are so clever
They like eating girls called Heather.

Witches think they are cute,
But really they look like a brute.

Witches think they are a nice friend,
They drive me round the bend.

Laura Jayne Steel (7)
Wiitherwack Primary School, Sunderland